Music

in Sweden

Göran Bergendal, Nils Hansson
Stig Jacobsson, Jan Kask
Dan Lundberg, Lars Westin

SVENSKA INSTITUTET

This publication was produced in collaboration with Rikskonserter
(Swedish Concert Institute).

© 1998 the authors and the Swedish Institute
Second printing
The authors alone are responsible for the opinions expressed in this publication.

EDITED BY Susanne Concha Emmrich (Svenska Institutet)
and Lena Roth (Rikskonserter)
TRANSLATED BY Cynthia Zetterqvist

COVER AND TYPOGRAPHY BY Linn Fleisher

TYPESETTING AND LAYOUT BY ReproAteljén, Skövde

PRINTED IN SWEDEN BY Grunditz & Forsberg Tryckeri AB, Lidköping 1998

ISBN 91-520-0503-8

Contents

Editors' preface

AFTER COLLABORATING earlier on a book about Swedish music which was published in two versions, in English and German, the Swedish Concert Institute has now decided, on the initiative of the Swedish Institute, to renew this collaboration.

The main reason for this publication is the fact that Stockholm has the opportunity to present itself as Cultural Capital of Europe during 1998. In order to illuminate and draw attention to different forms of culture in Sweden, the Swedish Institute is publishing a series of paperbacks in English, one of which is this book about music in Sweden.

The authors of each separate chapter were asked to describe the development in their particular field during the last two decades, but could go farther back in time when deemed necessary in order to refer to tradition and lines of development. "Art music" and "Jazz" therefore cover a longer period of time, without neglecting younger composers and musicians.

In order to give the reader the opportunity to "experience" Swedish music throughout the world, in other words, to listen to it, each chapter includes a discography. A presentation of Swedish artists has also been provided to complement this information. We hope you will enjoy reading this book and listening to Swedish music.

Contributors

Göran Bergendal (b. 1938) is a music journalist, radio man and music administrator. As head of development at the Swedish Concert Institute he has a special responsibility for contemporary music. Among other things he is the author of *33 svenska komponister* (33 Swedish composers, 1972) and *New Music in Iceland* (1991).

Nils Hansson (b. 1964) is music critic for *Dagens Nyheter*, Sweden's largest daily newspaper, and is responsible for covering rock and pop music.

After completing his university studies (BA in musicology, history of literature, theatre history, history of art), *Stig Jacobsson* (b. 1945) has worked as teacher and editor and is at present head of programme planning with the Norrköping Symphony Orchestra. He has written several books, including biographies of Dimitri Shostakovich, Carl Nielsen and Kurt Atterberg, as well as a history of Swedish music.

Jan Kask (b. 1949) is a music journalist. After studying musicology, aesthetics and German he worked as editorial assistant for Sohlman's music dictionary. He has been head of planning at Caprice Records and works at present as editor at the Swedish Concert Institute. He has written articles in scientific journals and in the National Encyclopaedia and has also been music critic for the Swedish daily newspaper *Svenska Dagbladet*.

Dan Lundberg (b. 1959) holds a PhD in musicology at the University of Stockholm. He specialises in cultural diversity and modern folk music. He has written several books and articles on Turkish, Eastern European and Scandinavian traditional music and also produced several radio programmes based on his work as an ethnomusicologist. He is also a well-known musician in the folk music field in Sweden.

Lars Westin (b. 1949) is a music journalist and record producer. Having worked for radio, television and numerous periodicals over the years, he is now the editor of *Orkester Journalen*, (the world's oldest jazz magazine, founded in 1933). He works at the programme department of the Swedish Concert Institute.

Swedish Art Music—openness and synthesis

MANY PEOPLE, particularly foreigners, often feel that there is something specifically "Swedish" in Swedish music, albeit impossible to pin down, just as it is impossible to say exactly what is so Finnish about Sibelius's music—it is more a question of emotional and associative qualities. So what is specifically Swedish in music? The slow movements of Berwald's symphonies? Or Adolf Fredrik Lindblad's songs? The music of August Söderman, Emil Sjögren, Wilhelm Stenhammar, Wilhelm Peterson-Berger and Kurt Atterberg—not to mention Hugo Alfvén's compositions and much of Lars-Erik Larsson's music—is definitely more national than cosmopolitan in flavour. The same applies to a certain extent to the music of Allan Pettersson, Ingvar Lidholm and Anders Eliasson.

Swedish music has generally been characterised by a considerable openness to fruitful influences, both from external sources and internally, from cross-fertilisation between different genres. Perhaps its essence lies in this more or less conscious mixture of domestic and foreign, of high and low culture, of simple and complex. At best it results in a synthesis which appears genuine and distinctive—individually coloured but of universal interest.

Sweden has always been heavily dependent on the import of musicians and ideas, right up to the present day. During the Baroque and Rococo eras and the golden, classical period of Gustav III, the musical language of a particular genre was relatively similar and generally established, regardless of whether the composer had been born abroad (Andreas Düben the Elder in the 1600s or Francesco Antonio Uttini, Johann Gottlieb Naumann, Abbé Vogler and Joseph Martin Kraus, all of whom were primarily known as opera composers, in the 1700s), in Sweden (Gustav Düben the Elder and his sons and Johan Wikmanson) or in what is now Finland (Bernhard Crusell). This explains why Johan Agrell (1701–65) could make a successful career for himself in Germany. A pupil of Johan Helmich Roman's, he was one of few exceptions: a Swedish composer who travelled in the opposite direction and was appointed composer to the court in Kassel and "Stadtmusikus" in Nuremberg.

The only early, significant and prolific exception was Johan Helmich Roman (1694–1758), the composer of *Drottningholms-musiken* (The Royal Wedding Music of Drottningholm), written for the wedding of Adolf Fredrik of Holstein-Gottorp and Frederick the Great's sister Lovisa Ulrika at Drottningholm Palace in 1744. Roman fully deserved the epithet "the Father of Swedish music". He was a versatile musician—a virtuoso on the violin, a conductor and a composer. As Kapellmeister of the court orchestra, he laid the foundation of an organised musical life in Sweden beyond the domains of the court with his public concerts before a paying audience in *Riddarhuset* (The House of the Nobility) in Stockholm in 1731. These were the first of their kind in Sweden and early even in comparison with the rest of Europe.

As an esteemed, Handel-influenced composer and Kapellmeister, he enlarged the repertoire with numerous compositions of his own, as well as introducing works by other composers which he collected on his travels in Europe. Roman's large output includes numerous orchestral sinfonias, suites (such as *Drottningholmsmusiken* and *The Golovin Music*) and concertos, as well as chamber music for various instrumental combinations and choral works (*The Swedish Mass*). With the aim of making the music more accessible to his audiences he adapted and modernised the Swedish language to fit the demands of the music. Strangely enough there is no portrait of Roman in existence.

The foundations of Sweden's institutionalised musical life came to be laid by Sweden's "enlightened despot", Gustav III, the founder of many important institutions (including the Royal Swedish Academy of Music in 1771 and the Royal Opera in 1773) for the promotion of a national musical life in Sweden.

The king himself took an active part in the work of the Royal Opera, engaging musicians and writing opera librettos in collaboration with authors such as Kellgren and composers such as Kraus (1755–92), who was known as "the Swedish Mozart". Like most of his more or less culturally-minded predecessors, including Gustav Vasa who founded the Royal Court Orchestra in 1526 as an autocratic manifestation of secular court music, King Erik XIV who even left fragments of his own compositions and Queen Christina and Adolf Fredrik, both of whom devoted themselves to raising the status of music at court, Gustav III was obliged to import nearly all his musicians and composers from abroad.

Carl Michael Bellman (1740–95) was the literary and musical all-round genius of 18th century Sweden—the author of a vast collection of songs, *Fredmans epistlar* (Fredman's Epistles) and *Fredmans sånger* (Fredman's Songs), which today are still as popular as ever. As a poet Bellman painted congenial pictures of society. At the same time (in the typical fashion of those times) he borrowed from other composers without compunction. During his lifetime he was a highly popular entertainer, and his art even gave him access to the court. Few people have succeeded in reflecting 18th century Stockholm—its inhabitants and their daily lives and social conditions—as well as Bellman did.

The Gustavian age of glory came to an abrupt end with the loss of Finland to Russia in 1809. Perhaps it was during the following century, with the growth of Romanticism which continued well into this century, that the intuitive rather than the intellectual aspect of the national interest began to be more in evidence.

Franz Berwald (1796–1868), like Roman, was launched by his father as a child prodigy on the violin, but he himself had greater ambitions as a composer. Even so he found it hard to adjust to the musical life of Sweden at that time, which in the absence of knowledgeable audiences and larger orchestras was mainly directed towards simple songs and chamber music more suited to the drawing-room. That Berwald's advanced formal language would have difficulty asserting itself was inevitable; his originality was considered "exaggerated" in a country where tastes were more inclined towards discretion and moderation. After a certain degree of success in Vienna in the 1840s Berwald returned to Stockholm, where he completed his *Sinfonie singulière* (No. 3) in March, 1845—which, however, did not receive its first performance until 1905. During certain periods he was forced to earn a living as an orthopaedist in Berlin and as manager of a glassworks in northern Sweden. With his four symphonies, his chamber music and his operas, Berwald still holds the most exalted position in 19th century musical Sweden, despite his modest successes during his lifetime. Apart from Allan

Pettersson from our own times, Berwald is still the only Swedish symphonist to have received international acclaim.

August Söderman (1832–76), who was mainly active as a choral composer and as a theatre musician in Stockholm (at the Royal Theatre, 1860–75), was a tremendously important stimulus for the whole of the ensuing National Romantic movement. The grandiose *Svenskt festspel* (Swedish Festival Music) was written in 1858 as the overture to the play *Några timmar på Kronoborgs slott* (A Few Hours at Kronoborg Castle), but was later used as the overture to Schiller's *Orleanska jungfrun* (The Maid of Orleans). The title "Svenskt festspel" was added later: although the music definitely sounds "Swedish", this was not in fact the composer's original intention with the work.

The opera conductor Ludvig Norman (1831–85) lived and worked in Stockholm parallel with Söderman. He was schooled in the spirit of Leipzig Romanticism surrounding Schumann, Mendelssohn and the Danish composer Gade, and he enthusiastically advocated these ideals in his many orchestral compositions and chamber music works. Norman is the most important Swedish symphonist between Berwald and Stenhammar. In the field of opera Ivar Hallström (1826–1901) and Andreas Hallén (1846–1925) were both prolific and successful. Emil Sjögren (1853–1918), who was influenced by Grieg and by French music, wrote songs and chamber music of high quality.

In his various roles as pianist, conductor and composer in Gothenburg and Stockholm and as a chamber music player throughout Sweden, Wilhelm Stenhammar (1871–1927) was one of the pioneers of the modern Swedish concert system. As a composer he was an aristocrat who had the common touch. Nevertheless, apart from a few exceptions, his rich output of chamber music and symphonic and vocal music has won the admiration of the experts rather than the hearts of the people. The two well-known *Sentimental Romances for violin and orchestra* were written in 1910, during the period that Stenhammar was principal conductor of the Gothenburg Symphony Orchestra. Together with the great *G minor symphony* and the two *piano concertos* they are his most loved works, apart from the hymn *Sverige* (Sweden), which has become something of a national anthem.

With their strong interest in Nordic literature, art and music, both Stenhammar and the Germanic Wilhelm Peterson-Berger (1867–1942) were strongly influenced by the Scandinavianism movement at the turn of the century, with its spiritual striving for common Nordic ideals which was a typical feature of that time. In the case of Peterson-Berger this was combined with a penchant for popular and provincial tradition—local culture and nature. As composers of musical dramas they were both strongly influenced by Beethoven and Wagner. Peterson-Berger also admired Sjögren and Grieg, while Stenhammar favoured his colleagues Carl Nielsen and, above all, Jean Sibelius. Despite Peterson-Berger's high-flown ambitions and the unassailable position of his opera *Arnljot* as Sweden's national opera, it was his small-scale works, in particular the volumes of lyrical piano miniatures which were published under the name of *Frösöblomster* (Frösö Flowers) and numerous part-songs, that were most successful.

Outside Sweden Hugo Alfvén (1872–1960) was best known in his day as the leader of the men's choir Orphei Drängar which he conducted on several tours, and as a successful symphonist. He made his breakthrough with *Svensk rapsodi nr 1 "Midsommarvaka"* (Swedish Rhapsody No. 1, Midsummer Vigil). *Midsummer Vigil* was inspired by a wedding in the

Stockholm archipelago in the 1890s, but was not completed until 1903 when Alfvén was staying in Skagen, Denmark, where he succeeded in capturing the heart of Maria, the wife of the Danish artist Severin Krøyer.

The work shows evidence of another typical symptom of that time, namely the ambition to be "Swedish" by referring to folk music and using transcriptions of folk tunes as the basis of a symphonically constructed rhapsody. The rhapsody was an immediate success internationally and has come to be regarded as a humorous and poetic song of praise to nature, to the Swedish summer and the Swedish temperament. Much later *Roslagsvår* (Roslag Spring) from the ballet *Den förlorade sonen* (The Prodigal Son) became something of an evergreen to many people, synonymous with the Swedish countryside.

The list of 20th century Swedish composers who were relatively well-known on the continent also includes such names as Kurt Atterberg (1887–1974), a brilliant master of orchestral colour whose symphonies were conducted by Nikisch, Furtwängler and Toscanini and whose operas were played in Germany (some of them were even premièred there), and Ture Rangström (1884–1947), a highly individual, expressionistic symphonist and writer of lyrical songs.

It was not until the appearance of Hilding Rosenberg and the rather late and somewhat tentative breakthrough of modernism in the 1920s that more radical and innovative means of expression were introduced, which were not consolidated until even later, by Karl-Birger Blomdahl and Ingvar Lidholm. Nevertheless, a large part of even the most recent Swedish music is still regarded by many people (probably non-Swedes for the most part) as "Swedish", despite its universal means of expression and its broader references. It would be impossible to imagine an Anders Eliasson in different cultural surroundings, just as the electro-acoustic music which is being produced in Sweden at the present time could not have developed anywhere else, any more than Sallinen's operas could have been written anywhere but in Finland. (J.K.)

THE BREAKTHROUGH OF MODERNISM

However, during the 1920s the break between late Romanticism's "national" stragglers and burgeoning modernism became unavoidable. Alongside the French-influenced expressionist Gösta Nystroem (1890–1966), Wilhelm Stenhammar's pupil Hilding Rosenberg (1892–1985) came to stand out more and more clearly, and for a long time to come, as the central figure of Swedish modernism. Nystroem composed *Ishavet* (The Arctic Ocean) for the Swedish Ballet in Paris, and with his *Sinfonia espressiva* he provided Swedish music of the 1930s with a counterpart to the heavy, at times machine-glorifying modernism of Rosenberg's *Symphony No. 2.* A pivotal work during the most threatening stage for Sweden of the Second World War was Rosenberg's monumental choral symphony *Johannes Uppenbarelse* (The Revelation of St. John) which also includes settings of poems by Hjalmar Gullberg.

The composer generation of the 1930s, which included Dag Wirén (1905–86), Lars-Erik Larsson (1908–86), Gunnar de Frumerie (1908–87) and Erland von Koch (b. 1910), focused more on a neo-classical style which gradually became more lyrical and romantic—even directly populistic at times during the war years. Larsson made his international breakthrough with the elegant *Stråksinfonietta* (Sinfonietta for Strings) in 1934, while the Romance from his *Pastoralsvit* (Pastoral Suite) could be seen as Sweden's answer to Samuel Barber's famous Adagio.

Larsson's cantata-like *Förklädd Gud* (God in Disguise) was written during the war year of 1940 to an evocative text by Hjalmar Gullberg. It contains much of the anguish of those times, clothed in archaic costume and saturated with a warm, Nordic tone. Wirén became known as a witty, elegant instrumental composer who could also write elegiac music, de Frumerie was primarily recognised as a writer of romantic songs and chamber music (his opera *Singoalla* was also highly successful), while Erland von Koch gradually came to adopt an idiom based on folk music in his unpretentious instrumental music. Hilding Hallnäs (1903–84), who lived and worked in Gothenburg, can also be numbered among this generation of composers, although his chamber music and orchestral works increasingly proved him to be more of an expressionist.

After the isolation of the war years there was an understandable curiosity and a need to catch up on what Sweden had missed out on: concurrently with internationalisation and the growth of the information society the national aspect became more diffuse. Nordic and European contacts which had been cut off now became tremendously important. Gösta Nystroem intensified his fundamentally weighty and expressive polyphony in works such as *Sinfonia del mare*. During the 1940s Rosenberg's personal, linear fusion of Palestrina, Bach, 1920s' expressionism and Sibelius was manifested in a number of monumental vocal works, which were followed in subsequent decades by an imposing collection of symphonies, operas, ballets, solo concertos and chamber music (mainly string quartets). In his role of father figure and mentor, in particular for the composer generation of the 1940s—the composers that came to form what was known as "The Monday Group"—Rosenberg has had a radical effect on craftsmanship, linear concepts and

KammarensembleN, a leading group for new music. Photo: Susanne Sandström

ethical issues, which has lasted until the end of this century.

The most important members of the composer group of the 1940s were Karl-Birger Blomdahl (1916–68), Sven-Erik Bäck (1919–94), Sven-Eric Johanson (1919–97) and Ingvar Lidholm (b. 1921), but it also included the eccentric Claude Loyola Allgén

(1920–90), whose music was totally neglected during his life-time, and Göte Carlid (1920–53), a composer who was well-informed about French and American modernism. In particular Blomdahl, Bäck and Lidholm later came to hold influential posts in Swedish musical life: Blomdahl as head of the music department at the Swedish Broadcasting Corporation, Bäck as head of the Edsberg Institute of Music (for a long time the Swedish Broadcasting Corporation's own post-graduate course for orchestral musicians and chamber music players) and Lidholm as head of the chamber music section at the Swedish Broadcasting Corporation and professor of composition at the Royal College of Music in Stockholm. Hindemith, Stravinsky, Dallapiccola, Schönberg, Bartók and Alban Berg constituted important points of departure for these composers, who, in a Europe in the throes of reconstruction, were fond of talking about spiritual regeneration and discussing the need for truth and contact in art. It was in this field of force that Eric Ericson, through his work with the Chamber Choir (and later also the Swedish Radio Choir and Orphei Drängar), laid the foundation of a Swedish choral culture of international esteem, which to a considerable degree has been associated with his name ever since.

In *Symphony No. 3, "Facettes",* and the orchestral work *Forma ferritonans,* Blomdahl developed a vital and fertile tonal language, characterised by serialism and metamorphosis technique. During the 1950s, in a legendary collaboration with the poet Erik Lindegren and the choreographer Birgit Åkesson, he expressed our experiences of those times in the ballet *Sisyphos,* the oratorio *I speglarnas sal* (In the Hall of Mirrors) and the internationally renowned "space opera" *Aniara.*

The Romantic Ingvar Lidholm can justly be described as

the most important composer in Sweden during the second half of this century. He has sublimated the waves of different styles from the continent—Stravinsky, Bartók, serialism, expressionism, pointillism, cluster technique—in a distinctive style of his own. Orchestral works such as *Ritornell, Motuscolores* and *Kontakion*, and major choral works such as *Skaldens natt* (The Night of the Poet) and *Nausikaa ensam* (Nausicaa Alone) and the two Strindberg operas *Holländarn* (The Dutchman) and *Ett Drömspel* (A Dream Play) show evidence of a range of expression and a naive, powerful elegance that is rare in Swedish music.

Both Sven-Erik Bäck and Sven-Eric Johanson came from a Free Church background. Their output is abundantly rich and varied and therefore not easily categorised, but on a superficial level they have several common characteristics. They introduced modernism into the theatre, the chamber and the church. Their combination of learning, Christian beliefs and musicianship provided fertile soil for music that included prayers as well as intellectual games. Bäck constantly referred to early music and, like Johanson, he emphasised in word and deed the social function of music. The main focus of their output is on chamber music and sacred choral music (Bäck's motets, for instance).

The post-war trends also made their mark on the composer generation of the 1930s. In symphonies, concertos and chamber music Wirén and Lars-Erik Larsson developed a metamorphosis technique reminiscent of a similar development in Denmark at that time (Holmboe, Niels Viggo Bentzon). The expression in Wirén's music became more profound, leaning towards Sibelius, while in 1960 Larsson began to experiment with a nonserial form of twelve-tone technique of his own. Hilding Hallnäs's encounter with post-war modernism resulted in a radical change of course towards dodecaphony and forceful expressiveness. At this time there were also three influential immigrant composers in Sweden who were the same age as the 1930s' generation: Eduard Tubin (1905–82) from Estonia, a notable symphonist and opera composer with a national basis, the Viennese Hans Holewa (1905–91), who introduced Schoenberg's twelve-tone technique to Sweden in the 1940s and whose own expressionistic chamber music and orchestral works attracted attention between the 1960s and the 1980s, and Werner Wolf Glaser (b. 1910), who was schooled in the Hindemith tradition.

Throughout the 1950s the composers in the Monday Group constituted a sort of mainstream regenerative force. However, there were two other schools in existence throughout this decade, one more conservative and one more radical. The conservative phalanx consisted of Jan Carlstedt (b. 1926), Hans Eklund (b. 1927), Bo Linde (1933–70) and to a certain extent Maurice Karkoff (b. 1927), all of whom had studied composition with Professor Lars-Erik Larsson. In their symphonies, concertos, chamber music and solo songs these composers formed a link with neo-classical composers such as Prokofiev, Hindemith, Britten and Shostakovich, even if expressiveness gradually came to dominate over naivety, and in Karkoff's case developed into a serial, at times decidedly fragmented and expressionistic style.

From the end of the 1940s important sources of information for the group of progressively-minded Swedish musicians were provided by the nightly relays from German radio stations of music by the continental avantgarde, as well as the famous International Summer Courses for New Music in Darmstadt with composers such as Messiaen, Stockhausen and Nono. Bengt Hambraeus (b. 1928) was a pioneer in Sweden

A studio at EMS, the centre for electro-acoustic music in Sweden. Photo: Josef Doukkali.

for timbrally conceived, serially permuted chamber music and orchestral music, sonoristic organ music (developed together with organist and composer Karl-Erik Welin) and, from 1955 onwards, electro-acoustic music (realised at the Westdeutscher Rundfunk studio in Cologne and RAI's studio in Milan). In 1972 Hambraeus emigrated to Canada where he was appointed professor of composition at McGill University in Montreal. He has subsequently tended towards a historicising postmodernism. Bo Nilsson (b. 1937), who comes from the ore-fields in Lapland, began his meteoric international career in his teens. For a few years, mainly during the 1950s and 1960s, he sublimated impressions from Stockhausen and Boulez into music that was both personal and highly artistic (his *Gösta Oswald cantatas* are pivotal works in Swedish music from this period).

Parallel with these contrasting streams, three widely differing symphonists were at work: the expressionistic Allan Pettersson (1911–80), whose sixteen monumental symphonies (often in one continuous movement) which plead the cause of the less fortunate have at last attracted considerable attention abroad; the intellectual, polemic and academically-oriented Gunnar Bucht (b. 1927), who was professor of composition and principal of the Royal College of Music in Stockholm, and Åke Hermanson (1923–96). In his sparsely textured orchestral works and chamber music, with its constant references to his childhood haunts in Bohuslän on the west coast of Sweden, Hermanson has developed a highly personal style, adopting a universal perspective which bears traces of Varèse and Xenakis, as well as classical symphonic writing and Nordic Romanticism.

Many of the composers who first made a name for themselves around 1960 had studied with Blomdahl or Lidholm. They also came under the influence (for shorter or longer periods) of international celebrities who visited Sweden, such as John Cage, Karlheinz Stockhausen, Mauricio Kagel, David Tudor and György Ligeti. They had roots in serial technique and post-Webern pointillistic texture and were also interested in cluster technique as practised by Ligeti and the Polish school. In addition some of them were influenced by the philosophy and music of John Cage, by American pop culture and by instrumental theatre. This generation of composers includes the legendary ensemble leader Siegfried Naumann (b. 1919) who in 1959 started out on a second career as a composer with Stockhausen as his guiding-star; Arne Mellnäs (b. 1933) who has composed diverting chamber music pieces and choral works (including international successes such as *Succsim*, *Aglepta* and *Dream*) and the opera *Doctor Glas* and the jazz trombonists Jan Bark (b. 1934) and Folke Rabe (b. 1935) who worked together, first in the Cul-

Daniel Börtz.

ture Quartet and then in the New Culture Quartet, using musical and other means to express social and cultural criticism (Rabe is also a much appreciated composer of choral and instrumental music). Further names from this generation are Karl-Erik Welin (1934–92), a pioneering organist and pianist and a naivistic Romantic composer, and Jan W Morthenson (b. 1940) who cultivated a puristic ideology of clusters and timbral clouds in the 1960s but switched in the 1970s to a stylistically pluralistic metamusic oriented towards social and cultural criticism. Lars Johan Werle (b. 1926) who was a pupil of Sven-Erik Bäck's, is one of the post-war period's most innovative and sensitive music dramatists who has been extremely successful with the arena opera *Drömmen om Thérèse* (The Dream about Thérèse), *Resan* (The Journey), *Tintomara* and *Animalen* (The Animal). He is also a significant choral composer (*Nautical Preludes*). The Hungarian-born composer Csaba Deak (b. 1932) has among other things enriched the repertoire of symphonic wind bands.

Around 1970 a number of composers became established who had studied with Ingvar Lidholm in Stockholm and who were also influenced by such figures as Ligeti and the Danish composer Per Nørgård: Sven-David Sandström (b. 1942), Daniel Börtz (b. 1943) and Anders Eliasson (b. 1947). The Hungarian-born composer Miklós Maros (b. 1943)—a brilliant orchestral composer—also belongs to this circle, as does Lars-Erik Rosell (b. 1944). Börtz's commitment to society has been an important source of strength to him. Inspired to a certain extent by Bruckner and with strong roots in the European tradition, Börtz stands out as the leading symphonist of his generation; his operas *Backanterna* (The Bacchae, directed by Ingmar Bergman) and *Marie Antoinette* (premièred in 1998) have attracted considerable attention. During the 1970s Sven-David Sandström made his international breakthrough with orchestral works and chamber music, employing strict rules of canon, microtones and a religious sphere of subjects. In the Requiem *De ur alla minnen fallna* (Mute the Bereaved Memories Speak) he gave free rein to a somewhat gaudy expressionism, after which he developed a post-modernistic, neo-romantic style in a steady flow of often highly successful ballets (together with choreographer Per Jonsson), operas, concertos, choral works and chamber music and the *High Mass*. Sandström has also been professor of composition at the Royal College of Music in Stockholm.

In contrast to the stylistic pluralism and exuberance of Sven-David Sandström's output, Anders Eliasson's music represents an unceasing, purposeful inward search. Primarily in chamber music and orchestral works—including *Il canto del vagabondo* (based on a passage from Carolus Linnaeus's *Iter lapponicum*), *Symphony No. 1* (awarded the Nordic Council Music Prize) and *Symphony No. 3* with obbligato part for alto saxophone—

he has developed a complex and organic style which displays powerful expressiveness, acuity, integrity, and a feeling for nature. Eliasson's style has an affinity with such widely differing composers as Ligeti, Brahms and Sibelius. One of his most notable choral works is a setting of Tomas Tranströmer's poem *Breathing room: July*.

Electro-acoustic music gained a foothold early on in Sweden due to the pioneering work of Rune Lindblad (1923–91) in Gothenburg and Bengt Hambraeus, Blomdahl and others in Stockholm. During the 1960s and 1970s a studio for electro-acoustic music was built in Stockholm (*EMS*) which at first was owned by the Swedish Broadcasting Corporation. *EMS* later became an independent foundation and since 1995 it has been a part of the Swedish Concert Institute. During the 1960s and 1970s the literary genre known as text-sound compositions attained a prominent position through Bengt Emil Johnson (b. 1936), Åke Hodell (b. 1919) and—not least—the versatile Lars-Gunnar Bodin (b. 1935). During the 1960s Ralph Lundsten (b. 1936) and Leo Nilsson (b. 1939) combined to compose milieu and exhibition music which caused quite a stir. Lundsten then continued in a more commercial vein with space effects and instrumental pastiches.

American minimalism, which has been cultivated by such composers as Steve Reich and John Adams, has not made much impact in Sweden. But it is possible to find structures that resemble minimalism in the music of several instrumental composers. One of these is Pär Lindgren (b. 1952), whose works for orchestra and ensembles are based on a technique of successive metamorphosis, masterly executed in the percussion concerto *Meander* and the orchestral work *Oaijé*, both of which are partly based on African rhythms. Klas Torstensson (b. 1951), who has

Anders Eliasson. Photo: Mats Lundkvist.

lived and worked in Holland since 1973, has won international acclaim with his works for orchestra and ensembles which have certain elements in common with Varèse and Xenakis as well as with minimalism. In several of his works Torstensson emphasises music's function as a physical activity. Mikael Edlund (b. 1950) combines minimalistic structures with an improvising musician's sensualism in his sparsely textured chamber music. Lars Sandberg (b. 1955) and the Zoltán Jeney pupil Peter Hansen (b. 1958) are two important exponents of an ascetic musical existentialism.

Post-modernistic pluralism and sensual elegance characterise the microtonally angular orchestral works *Clang and Fury* and *Celestial Mechanics* by Anders Hillborg (b. 1954), the sometimes introvert, sometimes spectacular concertos (*Motor Cycle Concerto* for trombone, for example) by the prolific, often consciously populistic Jan Sandström (b. 1954) and Johan Hammerth's (b. 1953) concertos for piano and percussion. The pol-

Karin Rehnqvist.
Photo: Lars Torndahl.

itically charged music of André Chini (born in France in 1945), which includes the violin concerto *Mururoa*, is considerably closer to Central European modernism.

A number of Swedish composers have focused on vocal music in various forms—not least in stylistically pluralistic music dramas. This list includes Hans Gefors (b. 1951), who studied with Per Nørgård in Denmark and who has composed the operas *Christina, Parken* (The Park) and *Vargen kommer* (The Wolf is Coming), all of which have attracted considerable attention; Thomas Jennefelt (b. 1954), who has written the operas *Gycklarnas Hamlet* (The Jesters' Hamlet) and *Farkosten* (The Vessel) as well as the major choral suite *Dichterliebe*, and Jonas Forssell (b. 1957), composer of the satirical refugee opera *Riket är ditt* (Thine is the Kingdom) which has also caused a considerable stir. Younger, stylistically independent opera composers include Reine Jönsson (b. 1960), Staffan Mossenmark (b. 1961), Peter Bengtson (b. 1961) and Carl Unander-Scharin (b. 1964).

Karin Rehnqvist (b. 1957) has received international acclaim for the vocal works *Davids Nimm, Solsången* (Song of the Sun) and *Puksånger — lockrop* (Timpanum Songs—Herding Calls). Her music is coloured to a considerable degree by her highly personal, unconventional and fresh approach to the Swedish folk music tradition. Mats Edén (b. 1957), who is a well-known folk musician, has also composed vocal music and chamber music works in the border zone between folk music and art music. Gunnar Valkare (b. 1943) has previously questioned the validity of Western modernism and has tried to find patterns for more informal music-making in the music of East Africa. Dror Feiler (b. 1951) emphasises his origin (he was born and grew up in Israel) and provides an alternative to Western aesthetics and means of expression with his brutalistic music.

There is a relatively large and influential circle of composers in Sweden who reject postmodernism and neo-romanticism on principle, and who instead link up with Central European modernism, as exemplified by Ferneyhough's structuralism, Donatoni's "mechanical" compositional methods and French spectral composition. Significant exponents of music with such points of departure are Ole Lützow-Holm (b. 1954), Christer Lindwall (b. 1950), Henrik Strindberg (b. 1954), Anders Hultqvist (b. 1955), Madeleine Isaksson (b. 1956), Chrichan Larsson (b. 1956), Göran Gamstorp (b. 1957) and Anders Nilsson (b. 1954)—whose *Symphony No. 1* in certain respects takes Beethoven's symphonic style as its starting point—as well as Kent Olofsson (b. 1962), Jonas Bohlin (b. 1963), Fredrik Ed (b. 1964), Fredrik Hedelin (b. 1965), Ivo Nilsson (b. 1966) and Per Mårtensson (b. 1967) among the younger generation. The list of composers who appear to be more independent in this respect includes Thomas Liljeholm (b. 1944), Johannes Jansson (b. 1950), Johannes Johansson (b. 1951), Rolf Martinsson (b. 1956), Lars Ekström

(b. 1956), Johan Jeverud (b. 1962) and Fredrik Österling (b. 1966).

During the 1980s and 1990s increased opportunities for the production of electro-acoustic music have been provided by the creation of a number of regional studios, mainly affiliated to the music colleges in Gothenburg, Malmö and Stockholm and also in Växjö. Swedish electro-acoustic music is highly esteemed in international circles. Contacts with France (IRCAM, Bourges), Great Britain and Canada have been particularly important factors for the development of *EMS*'s international network. A number of Swedish composers have contributed to the development of the genre—not only through traditional tape compositions but also through live electronics and music for multislide presentations: this list includes Tamas Ungvary (b. 1936), Tommy Zwedberg (b. 1946), who mainly works with analogue methods starting out from instrumental sounds, and Rolf Enström (b. 1951) whose name is associated with tape compositions such as *Slutförbannelser* (Final Curses) and the yoik adaptation *Tjidtjag-Tjidtjaggaise*, as well as multislide presentations (in collaboration with the photographer Thomas Hellsing). Other interesting composers include Pär Lindgren and Peter Lundén (both born 1955) who are noted for their well-constructed works for tape, Ragnar Grippe (b. 1951) who has developed an almost romantic world of sounds, William Brunson (b. 1953) and Anders Blomqvist (b. 1956), who have both created successful multislide presentations in collaboration with the photographer Josef Doukkali, and Bo Rydberg (b. 1960), who often composes in the border zone between electronics and instruments. Together with Anders Blomqvist, Åke Parmerud (b. 1953) has developed live electronics into a public art form. He has also won international acclaim with his brilliantly designed tape compositions saturated with meaningful content (as for example

Grains of Voices). In his large-scale tape compositions—mainly built up of concrete sounds and organ sounds—Ákos Rózmann (b. 1939) has created an intimate and highly personal musical world with an existential stamp. The younger generation of composers who mainly focus on electro-acoustic music includes Jens Hedman (b. 1962), Kim Hedås (b. 1965), Erik Mikael Karlsson (b. 1966) and Paulina Sundin (b. 1970). (G.B.)

DISCOGRAPHY BY STIG JACOBSSON

Sinfonias by AGRELL, HÖPKEN, JOHNSEN, ZELLBELL, WESSTRÖM, BRANT. National Museum Chamber Orchestra, Claude Génetay. Musica Sveciae MCDC 412.

Concertos by AGRELL, ZELLBELL, JOHNSEN. Maria Bania flute, Åsa Åkerberg cello, Lars Henriksson oboe, Mats Klingfors and Christian Beuse bassoon, Concerto Copenhagen, Andrew Manze. Musica Sveciae MCDC 411.

ROMAN: *The Swedish Mass*. The Adolf Fredrik Bach Choir, Drottningholm Baroque Ensemble, Anders Öhrwall. Musica Sveciae MSCD 401.

ROMAN: *The Royal Wedding Music of Drottningholm*. Uppsala Chamber Orchestra, Anthony Halstead. Naxos 8.553733.

ROMAN: *Flute Sonatas*. Penelope Evison flute, Eva Nordenfelt harpsichord, Olof Larsson and Kari Ottesen Baroque cello. Proprius PRCD 9019.

ROMAN: *Sinfonias and Violin Concertos*. Nils-Erik Sparf violin, Orpheus Chamber Ensemble. BIS-CD-284.

WIKMANSON: *Three String Quartets*. Nils-Erik Sparf, Per Sandklef violin, Björn Sjögren viola, Bengt Ericson cello. Musica Sveciae MSCD 402.

KRAUS: *Overture to "Olympie", Symphonies, Riksdag March*. Orchestra of the Age of Enlightenment, Anthony Halstead. Musica Sveciae MSCD 419.

KRAUS: *Funeral Music for Gustav III*. Soloists, Uppsala Academic Chamber Choir, Drottningholm Baroque Ensemble, Stefan Parkman. Musica Sveciae MSCD 416.

CRUSELL: *Three Clarinet Concertos*. Karl Leister clarinet, Lahti Symphony Orchestra, Osmo Vänskä. BIS-CD-345.

CRUSELL: *Three Clarinet Quartets*. Kari Krikku clarinet, Avanti Quartet. Ondine ODE 727.

BERWALD: *Three String Quartets*. Yggdrasil Quartet. BIS-CD-759.

BERWALD: *Four Symphonies, Konzertstück*. Christian Davidsson bassoon, Malmö Symphony Orchestra, Sixten Ehrling. BIS-CD-795/796.

BERWALD: *Overture to the Queen of Golconda, Piano Concerto, Violin Concerto, Tone Poems*. Marian Migdal piano, Arve Tellefsen violin, Royal Philharmonic Orchestra, Ulf Björlin. EMI 565073.

BERWALD: *Piano Quartet, Piano Trio No. 2, Septet*. The Gaudier Ensemble. Hyperion CD 66834.

BERWALD: *Piano Trios Nos. 1 & 3, Piano Quintet in C minor*. Berwald Quartet a.o. Musica Sveciae MSCD 521.

A F LINDBLAD: *Symphony No. 1, Songs*. Royal Stockholm Philharmonic Orchestra, Okko Kamu, MariAnne Häggander soprano, Mikael Samuelson baritone, Thomas Schuback piano. Caprice CAP 21425.

STENHAMMAR: *Songs*. Anne Sofie von Otter soprano, Bengt Forsberg piano, Håkan Hagegård baritone, Thomas Schuback piano. Musica Sveciae MSCD 623.

STENHAMMAR: *String Quartets Nos. 3 & 4*. Gotland Quartet. Musica Sveciae MSCD 602.

STENHAMMAR: *Symphonies Nos. 1 & 2, Piano Concertos Nos. 1 & 2, Incidental music, Serenade, Excelsior!, Florez and Blanzeflor, Two Sentimental Romances*. Gothenburg Symphony Orchestra, Neeme Järvi, Malmö Symphony Orchestra, Paavo Järvi a.o. BIS-CD-714-716.

STENHAMMAR: *Piano Music*. Niklas Sivelöv piano. Naxos 8.553730.

PETERSON-BERGER: *Songs*. Gunnel Bohman soprano, Thomas Lander baritone, Anders Kilström piano. Musica Sveciae MSCD 619.

PETERSON-BERGER: *Symphony No. 2, Violin Concerto.* Nilla Pierrou violin, Swedish Radio Symphony Orchestra, Stig Westerberg. Phono Suecia PSCD 95.

PETERSON-BERGER: *Symphony No. 3, Romance for Violin and Orchestra, Gullebarn's Lullabies.* Anne Sofie von Otter soprano, Mats Zetterqvist violin, Swedish Radio Symphony Orchestra, Siegfried Köhler. Musica Sveciae MSCD 630.

PETERSON-BERGER: *Frösö Flowers.* Lars Roos piano. Philips 426 987.

O LINDBERG: *Symphony in F major, Fiddler Per He Fiddled, Three Impressions of Travel.* Örebro Symphony Orchestra, Stig Westerberg. Sterling CDS 1015.

ANDRÉE: *Symphony No. 2, Fritiof Suite.* Stockholm Symphony Orchestra, Gustaf Sjökvist. Sterling CDS 1016.

T AULIN: *Violin Concerto No. 3,* STENHAMMAR: *Piano Concerto No. 2.* Christian Bergqvist violin, Greta Erikson piano, Swedish Radio Symphony Orchestra, Okko Kamu/Yevgeny Svetlanov. Musica Sveciae MSCD 622.

SJÖGREN: *Violin Sonata Nos. 1 & 2, Piano Sonata.* Leo Berlin violin, Greta Erikson, Lars Sellergren, Lars Roos piano. Swedish Society Discofil SCD 1028.

HÄGG: *Nordic Symphony, Amerikanische Festklänge, Concert Overtures Nos. 1 & 2.* Gävle Symphony Orchestra, Göran W Nilson/Mats Liljefors. Sterling CDS 1007.

WIKLUND: *Piano Concertos Nos. 1 & 2, Summer Night and Sunrise.* Ingemar Edgren, Greta Erikson piano, Gothenburg Symphony Orchestra, Jorma Panula, Swedish Radio Symphony Orchestra, Stig Westerberg. Caprice CAP 21363.

O OLSSON: *Symphony in G minor.* Gävle Symphony Orchestra, Mats Liljefors. Sterling CDS 1020.

O OLSSON: *Latin Hymns, Three Preludes and Fugues.* Eric Ericson Chamber Choir, Gunnar Idenstam organ. Musica Sveciae MSCD 611.

O OLSSON: *Requiem.* Soloists, Royal Stockholm Philharmonic Orchestra and Chorus, Anders Öhrwall. Caprice CAP 21368.

Swedish Piano Lyrics by FRYKLÖV, BECKMAN, ERIKSSON, HAQUINIUS, LUNDBERG. Dag Achatz piano. Musica Sveciae MSCD 628.

Chamber Music by ANDRÉE, NETZEL, T AULIN, MAIER, TEGNÉR. Bernt Lysell violin, Ola Karlsson cello, Lucia Negro piano, Tale Quartet. Musica Sveciae MSCD 528-529.

Cello Sonatas by NORMAN, J A HÄGG, KALLSTENIUS. Mats Lidström cello, Bengt Forsberg piano. Musica Sveciae MSCD 524.

Songs by PETERSON-BERGER, S VON KOCH, STENHAMMAR, RANGSTRÖM, ALFVÉN, SJÖGREN. Anne Sofie von Otter mezzosoprano, Bengt Forsberg piano. DG 449 189.

Songs for male-voice choir by O LINDBLAD, WENNERBERG, SÖDERMAN, PETERSON-BERGER, SVEDBOM, ALFVÉN, WIDÉEN, WIKANDER. Orphei Drängar (The Sons of Orpheus), Eric Ericson. Proprius PRCD 9046.

Swedish Ballads by SÖDERMAN, PETERSON-BERGER, STENHAMMAR, RANGSTRÖM. Ingvar Wixell baritone, Royal Stockholm Philharmonic Orchestra, Johan Arnell. Musica Sveciae MSCD 617.

STENHAMMAR: *Violin Sonata,* T AULIN: *Four Aquarelles,* KALLSTENIUS: *Violin Sonata.* Nils-Erik Sparf violin, Bengt Forsberg piano. Musica Sveciae MSCD 616.

ALFVÉN: *Symphony No. 3, Swedish Rhapsody No. 3 (Dalecarlia Rhapsody).* Royal Stockholm Philharmonic Orchestra, Nils Grevillius/Stig Westerberg. Swedish Society Discofil SCD 1008.

ALFVÉN: *Symphony No. 4.* Elisabeth Söderström soprano, Gösta Winbergh tenor, Royal Stockholm Philharmonic Orchestra, Stig Westerberg. Bluebell ABCD 001.

ALFVÉN: *Songs for male-voice choir.* Orphei Drängar (The Sons of Orpheus), Robert Sund. BIS-CD-633.

ALFVÉN: *Swedish Rhapsodies Nos. 1, 2 & 3 (Midsummer Vigil, Dalecarlia Rhapsody & Uppsala Rhapsody), Legend of the Skerries, The Mountain King.* Royal Stockholm Philharmonic Orchestra, Neeme Järvi. BIS-CD-725.

RANGSTRÖM: *Songs.* Birgitta Svendén mezzo-soprano, Håkan Hagegård baritone, Thomas Schuback piano. Musica Sveciae MSCD 629.

RANGSTRÖM: *Symphony No. 1, Dithyramb, Spring Hymn.* Norrköping Symphony Orchestra, Michail Jurowski. cpo 999 367.

RANGSTRÖM: *Miss Julie, Advent, Divertimento elegiaco, From King Erik's Songs, Legends of the Lake Mälaren, Songs.* Orchestra of the Royal Opera, Varujan Kodijan, Stig Westerberg, Elisabeth Söderström soprano, Erik Sædén baritone, Kerstin Meyer soprano, Lars Roos piano. Swedish Society Discofil SCD 1040.

ATTERBERG: *Symphony No. 2, Suite No. 3.* Mircea Saulesco violin, Gideon Roehr viola, Swedish Radio Symphony Orchestra, Stig Westerberg. Swedish Society Discofil SCD 1006.

ATTERBERG: *Symphony No. 3, Horn Concerto.* Royal Stockholm Philharmonic Orchestra, Sixten Ehrling, Albert Linder horn, Gothenburg Symphony Orchestra, Gérard Oskamp. Caprice CAP 21364.

ATTERBERG: *Symphony No. 6, A Värmland Rhapsody, Ballade Without Words.* Norrköping Symphony Orchestra, Jun'ichi Hirokami. BIS-CD-533.

NYSTROEM: *Sinfonia del Mare, Sinfonia concertante.* Elisabeth Söderström soprano, Erling Blöndal Bengtsson cello, Swedish Radio Symphony Orchestra, Stig Westerberg. Swedish Society Discofil SCD 1015.

NYSTROEM: *Sinfonia Seria, Ishavet, Sinfonia breve.* Royal Stockholm Philharmonic Orchestra, Jukka-Pekka Saraste, Peter Erös, Gothenburg Symphony Orchestra, Sixten Ehrling. Caprice CAP 21332.

ROSENBERG: *Symphony No. 2, Marionettes, Louisville Concerto.* Royal Stockholm Philharmonic Orchestra, Herbert Blomstedt, London Symphony Orchestra, Sixten Ehrling, Swedish Radio Symphony Orchestra, Stig Westerberg. Swedish Society Discofil SCD 1026.

ROSENBERG: *Symphonies Nos. 3 & 6.* Royal Stockholm Philharmonic Orchestra, Herbert Blomstedt, Stockholm Symphony Orchestra, Stig Westerberg. Phono Suecia PS 100.

ROSENBERG: *Symphony No. 4.* Håkan Hagegård baritone, Swedish Radio Choir, Gothenburg Symphony Orchestra, Sixten Ehrling. Caprice CAP 21429.

ROSENBERG: *String Quartets Nos. 4 & 7, Moments Musicaux.* Fresk Quartet, Berwald Quartet, Gotland Quartet. Caprice CAP 21353.

TUBIN: *Symphony No. 5, Kratt (The Goblin).* Bamberg Symphony Orchestra, Neeme Järvi. BIS-CD-306.

PETTERSSON: *Symphony No. 6.* Deutsches Symphonie-Orchester Berlin, Manfred Trojahn. cpo 999 124.

PETTERSSON: *Symphonies Nos. 7 & 11.* Norrköping Symphony Orchestra, Leif Segerstam. BIS-CD-580.

LARSSON: *Saxophone Concerto, Divertimento, Horn Concertino, Quattro Tempi, String Quartet No. 3.* Christer Johnsson saxophone, Swedish Radio Symphony Orchestra, Leif Segerstam, Stockholm Sinfonietta, Jan-Olav Wedin, Ib Lanzky-Otto horn, Stockholm Quartet a.o. Caprice CAP 21492.

LARSSON: *God Disguised, Pastoral Suite, Violin Concerto.* Hillevi Martinpelto soprano, Håkan Hagegård baritone, Erland Josephson recitation, Arve Tellefsen violin, Swedish Radio Symphony Orchestra, Esa-Pekka Salonen. SONY SK 64140.

E VON KOCH: *Lapland Metamorphoses, Impulsi, Echi, Ritmi, Oxberg Variations.* Royal Stockholm Philharmonic Orchestra, Stig Westerberg. Swedish Society Discofil SCD 1024.

E VON KOCH: *Saxophone Concerto, Scandinavian Dances, Nordic Capriccio, Swedish Dance Rhapsody, Characters.* Sigurd Raschèr saxophone, Munich Philharmonic Orchestra, Swedish Radio Symphony Orchestra, Stig Westerberg. Phono Suecia PSCD 55.

FRUMERIE: *Pastoral Suite, Songs, Piano Trio No. 2* Börje Mårelius flute, Swedish Radio Symphony Orchestra, Stig Westerberg, Kerstin Meyer mezzo-soprano, Jan Eyron piano a.o. Swedish Society Discofil SCD 1022.

WIRÉN: *Serenade for Strings, Cello Concerto, Divertimento, Piano Concerto.* Mats Rondin cello, Mats Widlund piano, Swedish Chamber Orchestra, Peteri Sakari. Caprice CAP 21513.

WIRÉN: *Symphony No. 4, Music for Strings, Serenade for Strings, Sinfonietta.* Swedish Radio Symphony Orchestra, Sixten Ehrling, Royal Stockholm Philharmonic Orchestra, Stig Westerberg, Örebro Chamber Orchestra, Lennart Hedwall. Swedish Society Discofil SCD 1035.

WIRÉN: *String Quartets Nos. 2 & 5, Quartet, Little Serenade.* Ferro Quartet, Per Skareng guitar a.o. Caprice CAP 21413.

34

BÄCK: *String Quartets Nos. 2 & 4, String Quintet, Flute Sonata, Expansive Preludes, Favola.* Crafoord Quartet, Berwald Quartet, Manuela Wiesler flute, Arne Torger piano a.o. Caprice CAP 21490.

HAMBRAEUS: *Rota II, Symphonia Sacra, Ricordanza.* Norrköping Symphony Orchestra, Francis Travis, McGill Chamber Singers a.o. Caprice CAP 21421.

LUNDQVIST: *Symphony No. 1, The Arctic, Call, Siebenmal Rilke.* Sara Olsson soprano, Umeå Symphony Orchestra, B Tommy Andersson. Bluebell ABCD 072.

M KARKOFF: *Symphonies Nos. 4 & 7, Pezzi, 6 Chinese Impressions, Vision, Serious Songs.* Swedish Radio Symphony Orchestra, Stig Westerberg, Kerstin Meyer soprano, Royal Stockholm Philharmonic Orchestra, Sixten Ehrling. Swedish Society Discofil SCD 1923.

EKLUND: *Music for Orchestra, Fantasia, String Quartet No. 3, Small Talk.* Swedish Radio Symphony Orchestra, Stig Westerberg, Åke Olofsson cello, Norrköping Quartet a.o. Swedish Society Discofil SCD 1038.

LINDE: *Symphony No. 2, Violin Concerto, Pensieri.* Ulf Wallin violin, Norrköping Symphony Orchestra, Jun'ichi Hirokami. BIS-CD-621.

Oboe Concertos by ROMAN, LARSSON, E VON KOCH, LINDE. Mårten Larsson oboe, Camerata Roman. Intim Music IMCD 033.

WIRÉN: *String Quartets Nos. 2 & 4,* LINDE: *String Quartet,* BÖRTZ: *String Quartet No. 3.* Fresk Quartet, Slovak Quartet, Gotland Quartet. Phono Suecia PSCD 18.

BOLDEMANN: *Lieder der Vergänglichkeit, Epitaphs, Notturno, Sinfonietta.* Håkan Hagegård baritone, Sylvia Lindenstrand mezzo-soprano, Birgit Nordin soprano, Swedish Radio Symphony Orchestra, Berislav Klobucar. Phono Suecia PSCD 29.

Choral Music by BÄCK, L EDLUND, MELLNÄS, MAROS. Eric Ericson Chamber Choir, Eric Ericson. Phono Suecia PSCD 38.

Piano Music by L OLSSON, HÄGG, FRYKLÖF, ALMÉN, HAQUINIUS, ERIKSSON, MORALES, MILVEDEN, MANKELL. Bengt Forsberg piano. Acoustica ACCD-1014.

BLOMDAHL: *Dance Suites Nos. 1 & 2, Clarinet Trio, In the Hall of Mirrors.* Royal Stockholm Philharmonic Orchestra, Swedish Radio Choir, Sixten Ehrling a.o. Caprice CAP 21424.

BLOMDAHL: *Symphony No. 3, "Facettes", Sisyphus, Forma Ferritonans, ...The Journey on this Night.* Royal Stockholm Philharmonic Orchestra, Sixten Ehrling, Antal Dorati, Sergiu Comissiona, Elisabeth Söderström soprano, Yuri Ahronovich. Caprice CAP 21365.

LIDHOLM: *Greetings from an old World, Toccata e Canto, Kontakion, Ritornell.* Royal Stockholm Philharmonic Orchestra, Gennady Rozhdestvensky. Chandos CHAN 9231.

LIDHOLM: *Poesis, Rites, Ritornell.* London Symphony Orchestra, Sixten Ehrling, Royal Stockholm Philharmonic Orchestra, Hans Schmidt-Isserstedt. Swedish Society Discofil SCD 1027.

LIDHOLM: *A Dream Play.* Håkan Hagegård baritone, Hillevi Martinpelto soprano a.o. Orchestra and Chorus of the Royal Opera, Kjell Ingebretsen. Caprice CAP 22029.

LIDHOLM: *Laudi, Canto LXXXI, ...a riveder le stelle,* WERLE: *Canzone 126, Trees.* Stockholm Chamber Choir, Eric Ericson. Phono Suecia PSCD 35.

MALMLÖF-FORSSLING: *Flowings, Aum, Ahimsa, Silver Quartet, Albero, Reluce, Shanti chanti.* Royal Stockholm Philharmonic Orchestra, Neeme Järvi, Märta Schéle soprano, Allmänna Sången, Cecilia Rydinger Alin, Gävle Symphony Orchestra, Grzegorz Nowak. Bluebell ABCD 069.

NILSSON: *Brief an Gösta Oswald, Drei Szenen, Stunde eines Blocks.* Berlin Radio Symphony Orchestra, Francis Travis, Swedish Radio Symphony Orchestra, Herbert Blomstedt, Jukka-Pekka Saraste, Leif Segerstam, Dorothy Dorow soprano. Phono Suecia PSCD 33.

ELIASSON: *Canto del vagabondo, Canti in lontananza, La fièvre, Disegno per Quartetto d'archi.* Swedish Radio Symphony Orchestra, Herbert Blomstedt, Stig Westerberg, Stockholm Wind Quintet, Crafoord Quartet. Caprice CAP 21402.

ELIASSON: *Symphony No. 1, Bassoon Concerto, Ostacoli.* Knut Sönstevold bassoon, Ostrobothnian Chamber Orchestra, Juha Kangas, USSR Ministry of Culture Symphony Orchestra, Gennady Rozhdestvensky. Caprice CAP 21381.

S-D SANDSTRÖM: *The High Mass*. Lena Hoel, Marianne Eklöf a.o. Swedish Radio Choir, Swedish Radio Symphony Orchestra, Leif Segerstam. Caprice CAP 22036.

S-D SANDSTRÖM: *Flute Concerto, Lonesome, Cello Concerto*. Tobias Carron flute, Magnus Andersson guitar, Torleif Thedéen cello, Swedish Radio Symphony Orchestra, Leif Segerstam. Caprice CAP 21418.

BÖRTZ: *Sinfonias Nos. 1 & 7, Strindberg Suite, Parodos*. Royal Stockholm Philharmonic Orchestra, Gennady Rozhdestvensky. Chandos CHAN 9473.

BÖRTZ: *The Bacchae*. Sylvia Lindenstrand, Peter Mattei a.o. Orchestra of the Royal Opera, Kjell Ingebretsen. Caprice CAP 22028.

M EDLUND: *brains and dancin', Trio Sol, Orchids in the Embers, Small Feet, Leaves, Fantasy on a Town*. Fagéus Trio, Stefan Bojsten piano, Magnus Andersson guitar, Mats Widlund piano a.o. Phono Suecia PSCD 20.

HILLBORG: *Clang and fury, Lamento, Celestial Mechanics, Haut-Posaune*. Swedish Radio Symphony Orchestra, Esa-Pekka Salonen, Eric Ericson Chamber Choir, Christian Lindberg trombone. Phono Suecia PSCD 53.

J SANDSTRÖM: *Motor Cycle Concerto*. Christian Lindberg trombone, Swedish Radio Symphony Orchestra, Leif Segerstam. BIS-CD-538.

REHNQVIST: *Davids Nimm, Sudden Changes, Time of Taromir, Timpanum Songs–Herding Calls, Lamento–Vibrations of a Voice*. Ostrobothnian Chamber Orchestra, Juha Kangas, Royal Stockholm Philharmonic Orchestra, Göran W Nilson. Phono Suecia PSCD 85.

ENSTRÖM: *Directions, Tjidtjag and Tjidtjaggaise, Final Curses*. Electro-acoustic music. Caprice CAP 21374.

Electro-acoustic music by HAMBRAEUS, MORTHENSON, HANSON, HODELL, BÄCK, BODIN, R LINDBLAD, UNGVARY, JOHNSON, RÓZMANN, LINDGREN, ENSTRÖM, PARMERUD, BLOMQVIST, ZWEDBERG. Phono Suecia PSCD 41.

Electro-acoustic music by BODIN, PARMERUD, BÄCK, SÖDERBERG, UNGVARY, LUNDÉN, BLOMQVIST, GRIPPE, KARLSSON, ENSTRÖM, BRUNSON, HELLSTRÖM, RYDBERG, RÓZMANN. Caprice CAP 21471.

Folk Music—from village greens to concert platforms

DURING THE second half of the twentieth century folk music has undergone a radical transformation, both concerning the sound of the music and the form itself—what we regard as folk music. Folk music has also attained a new status in the musical life of Sweden, which is largely due to the rise in interest during the 1970s and 1980s. Perhaps the most vital difference is that young people are now playing folk music to a far greater extent than before.

The roles of the musicians have also changed, due to new demands that have been made, both on the music itself and on the musicians. Folk music is constantly being adapted to new media and new surroundings. We no longer necessarily find the "typical" folk musician playing dance music at a wedding. We are equally likely to find him leading a study group, lecturing at a music college, performing on a concert platform or making a CD in a recording studio. It is also quite likely that the folk musician is not a he but a she. Roughly speaking, among the younger generations in Sweden today as many female as male musicians play folk music, which is a big difference compared to earlier times. The changed roles of the musicians are also reflected in how the players see themselves. Do they think of themselves as *spelmän* (the Swedish term for a traditional folk musician), as musicians or as folk musicians if they play arrangements of folk music on modern instruments, such as electric guitar, synthesiser or saxophone, in a group?

Folk music at Övre Gärdsjö during the Lake Siljan Festival 1995.
Photo: Per-Ulf Allmo.

That an increasing number of players within the new, popular folk music domains choose to call themselves folk musicians reflects a new attitude, not only towards their own identity as folk musicians but also towards the music itself.

Today we have a situation where folk music is used and created by people with very varied backgrounds. We have a rich, flourishing fiddlers' tradition which is perpetuated by older Swedish fiddlers as well as by a new generation of technically skilled players who have a solid musical training behind them. In addition to the individual musicians, folk groups have also become a common sight on Sweden's musical platforms.

The new styles and forms of ensemble-playing that have emerged since the 1960s are related to the development of the music industry; the opportunities for getting to know music, both modern and traditional, from other cultures, are greater than ever before. During the 1980s and 1990s in particular, folk music has been characterised by enthusiastic experimenting which has widened its domains in many different directions. New instruments, new combinations and influences from other genres and cultures have all made their mark on modern Swedish folk music.

ON THE ROAD TO WORLD MUSIC

How and why have these changes taken place? The first step was taken when traditional fiddlers' music began to attract attention at the beginning of this century. Folk music arenas changed and many fiddlers became concert platform performers, exchanging the barn and the village green for the community centre or the village hall. As a result of the romantic folk music ideal which prevailed during the early twentieth century, these concert performers were transformed from dance musicians to tradition-bearing symbols of the old agrarian society.

With the development of *spelmanslag* (fiddlers' groups) during the 1940s, a new type of organised folk music emerged. The most influential trend-setter was the Rättvik Spelmanslag whose signature tune, *Gärdebylåten* (The Gärdeby Tune), became Sweden's first folk music hit, thanks to the mass media. Through radio broadcasts and gramophone recordings *Gärdebylåten* became something of a national plague towards the end of the 1940s.

The Swedish Broadcasting Corporation's interest in folk music during the 1940s and 1950s (mainly represented by producer and folk music collector Matts Arnberg) was an important factor which contributed to the continued dissemination and development of folk music in the country. By 1950, the Swedish Broadcasting Corporation had issued seventeen

78 rpm records with traditional Swedish folk music.

When ensembles were formed in the 1970s with musical instruments with different functions (melody, bass, harmony, rhythm), they were regarded as an innovation in Sweden. However, this type of ensemble can be found all over Europe in urban forms of folk music and popular music which have developed since the nineteenth century; Greek rebetico ensembles, Hungarian gypsy bands and Rumanian lautar orchestras are all examples of this modern folk music tradition. But there are also Swedish counterparts. The twentieth century *gammaldansband* (old-time dance bands) with a basic combination of accordion, double bass, and guitar are in many ways analogous to the European ensembles.

For the most part, as the name implies, the repertoire of these ensembles is based on old-time dances—popular Swedish dances from the beginning of this century. Carl Jularbo (1893–1966) is perhaps the most influential trend-setter in this context; between 1913 and 1960 he was Sweden's best selling gramophone artist. Many of his most popular melodies were adaptations of folk melodies (A complete discography of Carl Jularbo's gigantic production of 1,576 titles by Björn Englund was published with an English commentary in 1992: The National Archives of Recorded Sound and Moving Images, Swedish Discography No. 8). However, this type of band has never seriously come under consideration as a part of the Swedish folk music tradition.

The reason why old-time dance music has never been regarded as "proper" folk music goes back to the romantic folk music ideal which was prevalent among folk music collectors during the nineteenth and early twentieth centuries. For various reasons the nineteenth century fiddlers' tradition was regarded as central to the folk music concept, or, rather, it became the guiding rule for what it should comprise.

Many types of music that from a functional perspective ought to constitute the natural development of the fiddlers' tradition have thereby ended up outside what is usually counted as folk music. Modern dance band music is perhaps one of the most obvious examples. The function of modern dance band music ought reasonably to correspond exactly with most definitions of folk music. Nevertheless, it definitely ends up on the outside.

Old-time dance bands and their repertoire evidently border on folk music, but are nevertheless not acknowledged as "proper" folk music in Sweden. In the following discussion, when we examine the development of ensemble-playing in modern Swedish folk music, we should bear in mind the fact that we are talking about a musical field which is limited by a very narrow definition of folk music.

FOLK MUSIC AND JAZZ

The second step, after the old-time dance bands, towards the folk music bands of today is to be found in the Swedish folk music-based jazz of the 1960s. A highly significant event in this context was the recording of the radio programme, "Jazz and folk music—a musical adventure".

On the initiative of the Swedish Broadcasting Corporation and the Swedish Centre for Folk Song and Folk Music Research, four Swedish jazz musicians and bandleaders were commissioned to make arrangements of folk music recordings which were preserved in the Swedish radio's folk music archives. The programme became Sweden's contribution to *Triumph Varieté* in Monte Carlo in 1965, where it was awarded the prize for the best entertainment programme. Parts of the programme were issued on an LP, *Adventures In Jazz And Folklore*.

The manner in which the musicians and arrangers adapted and made use of the folk music material was unique. In earlier folk music adaptations by art music composers, the starting point was a notated melody which was varied and harmonised. This time several folk music recordings were used directly in the arrangements.

The tune which has probably been most widely distributed was originally collected by the musicologist Matts Arnberg on one of the Swedish Broadcasting Corporation's recording excursions in the late 1950s. It was sung by Hilma Ingberg, a Finno-Swedish singer. The text of this comic song, which today is familiar to most Swedes, goes: *I fjol så gick jag med herrarna i hagen ... I år har jag något som sparkar i magen* (Last year I went with the lads to the meadow ... This year I've got something kicking in my tummy"). The jazz pianist Jan Johansson made an arrangement of the song which begins with the whole recording of Hilma Ingberg singing, after which the orchestra gradually takes over.

It is interesting to note that this technique has come to be regarded as an innovation in the media's "folk pop" world of the 1990s. For example, when today's ethno-techno musicians use sampled folk music, the technical conditions are obviously very different, but the principle is nevertheless the same.

Much of what is new in the modern folk music that we are discussing here has its origin in the fact that the music has been transferred from one context—one arena—to another. During the nineteenth century it was possible to observe throughout Europe how folk music moved from the country to the towns, just as the performers moved from village greens to concert platforms. We can see *Adventures In Jazz And Folklore* as another type of move, which in all probability is irreversible: the exchange of one musical form of existence for another—from live music to medialised music. In Jan Johansson's arrangement, moreover, this is a two-stage process: firstly, the result of the music-making lives on in the form of a recording, besides which we have the interesting fact that the recording itself is based on earlier recordings. This is arguably the most significant change in music-making and musicians' attitudes in most camps during the 1990s. Music now has <u>two</u> forms of existence: music transmitted by the media and live music, and both forms are in a state of permanent symbiosis.

Secondly, *Adventures In Jazz And Folklore* also represents a step in another, more long-term, process of transformation. When folk music was fashionable in nineteenth century Stockholm, the music was not performed by the tradition-bearers themselves but by trained singers. Here *Adventures In Jazz And Folklore* represents the first step in a development where folk musicians themselves take centre place on the artistic stage and experiment with their own music. In *I fjol så gick jag med herrarna i hagen* the tradition-bearer is part of the recording, but does not take part in the actual music-making. Obviously the next step is to bring the folk musicians themselves into the recording studio.

FOLK MUSIC AND POP

This next stage of development is represented here by a collaboration between the folk music group Skäggmanslaget and the pop group Contact, which in 1970 resulted in a recording of *Gråtlåten, polska efter Hjort Anders* (The Crying Tune, polska after Hjort Anders) on Skäggmanlaget's LP *Pjål, gnäll och ämmel*

44

(Squeaks, Squawks and Whimpers) which in many ways was epoch-making.

Skäggmanslaget consisted of three young folk musicians: Wilhelm Grindsäter, Thore Härdelin and Petter Logård. Contact, on the other hand, was a Stockholm-based pop group with organist and singer Ted Ström as the driving force. Their models were probably to be found in British "folk rock" which had developed during the 1960s. This "musical encounter" was also the result of an external initiative, this time from the Youth Department of the Swedish Broadcasting Corporation.

The encounter between Skäggmanslaget and Contact thus resulted in a recording of *Gråtlåten* which was an immediate success in the Swedish hit charts. The record *Pjål, gnäll och ämmel* received the Swedish Gramophone Award in 1970.

The popularity of Skäggmanslaget can be explained in a number of ways.

Firstly, due to political currents in society, such as the "green wave" and the "alternative movement", a new folk music audience had emerged that could identify with the music and the musicians. Folk music and rock stood for alternatives to established music, a non-commercial music. Folk music could also stand for "the people's music", which fitted in well with the world of ideas of left-wing politics.

Secondly, the change of attitude towards music and musicians during the 1970s resulted in a more liberal view of renewal and the opinion (which is more relevant in this context) that anyone, regardless of whether he or she is a tradition-bearer or not, has the right to use folk music. Thirdly, among their audience in the young folk music generation Skäggmanslaget were respected as skilful musicians, a reputation which should not be underestimated. A fourth explanation of the popularity of *Gråtlåten* was that it fell onto good ground among key figures at the Swedish Broadcasting Corporation.

From this vantage point we can continue with a further comparison between Jan Johansson's version of *I fjol så gick jag med herrarna i hagen* and *Gråtlåten*. Both arrangements are obviously characterised by the encounter or "clash" between two musical worlds. As a listener one has a definite feeling that the musicians see the original melodies as they are performed by the tradition-bearers (Hilma Ingberg and Skäggmanslaget, respectively) as starting points for the arrangements. This is evident in the fact that the "original" melodies are heard before the jazz musicians and pop musicians begin to play.

It is possible that *Gråtlåten* was inspired by the arrangement of *I fjol så gick jag med herrarna i hagen*, but this is not particularly likely. It is more probable that the similarities between the two arrangements are partly due to the fact that the musicians felt a great respect for the original versions and partly because by beginning with the original the transformation stood out more clearly and was even more effective. At the same time we should not forget the explanation which is nearest to hand, namely that this type of construction is commonly used both in jazz and popular music.

NEW FOLK MUSIC INSTRUMENTS

If we continue to follow new trends in modern Swedish folk music by examining new ensemble types and new ways of playing together, the 1980s could arguably be described as the decade of the instruments. A great number of new folk music groups appeared in the 1980s, inspired among other things by groups from Ireland, Hungary and the Balkans (and of course by other contemporary Swedish groups).

46

Two influential groups from this decade were Filarfolket (1980–90) and Groupa (1980–). What above all distinguished the sound of these groups from earlier folk music bands was the use of wind instruments (saxophones, clarinets and trumpets) in combination with percussion (mainly miscellaneous striking apparatus with folk music origins). With woodwind and percussion in the foreground, Filarfolket experimented with "riffs" (rhythmic and melodic ostinati) as an accompaniment to folk tunes.

The new common denominator in these groups was the great variety of instruments; several of the players were also multi-instrumentalists. It is noticeable that the separation between the "original" folk music version and the "new" version which was clearly distinguishable in the arrangements of *Gråtlåten* and *I fjol så gick jag med herrarna i hagen* is less in evidence or lacking entirely.

The ideological grounding which was brought about by the folk music vogue of the 1960s and 1970s meant that in the midst of these enthusiastic experiments there was still a strong determination to perpetuate tradition. However the new instruments brought problems concerning intonation and rhythm in folk music into focus in a different way from before.

POLSKA ON THE BOUZOUKI

During the 1980s many new instruments, such as bouzouki and mandola, bass clarinet and contrabass clarinet, berimbau and various sorts of saxophones etc, were introduced into Swedish folk music. The musicians in Filarfolket and Groupa became the idols of the young folk musicians of the decade.

It is probably also true to say that trend-setters among the folk musicians of the 1980s played a more active role in the transformation of folk music-making than their predecessors in the 1960s and 1970s, in particular since folk music now had an established place at music colleges and folk high schools, and many musicians who were actively involved in folk music were called upon as experts. Many young folk musicians studied musicology and ethnology and were involved in the collection and publication of folk music material.

DRONE ROCK

As mentioned previously, folk music and folk music-making have undergone radical change. The Swedish group Hedningarna is one example of this new situation.

Hedningarna was formed in 1986–87 by three musicians, Anders Stake, Björn Tollin and Totte Mattsson. From the start the group was oriented towards a historic sound ideal. The basic instruments of the group were bagpipe, Mora fiddle (*Moraharpa*, an older form of keyed fiddle) and modified Renaissance lute, in combination with various types of simple percussion instruments. Their ensemble-playing was based on three simple building blocks: melody, drone and rhythm.

By the end of the 1980s the group had built up a "medieval image". Concerts were planned down to the last detail. "During the concerts in the Folk Music Tent project in 1990 we hit upon the 'show'—a bit of hocus-pocus, incense and lighting", Totte Mattson explained in an interview in 1995.

During the autumn of 1990 Hedningarna began to collaborate with two female Finnish singers, Sanna Kurki-Suonio and Tellu Paulasto, who specialised in an archaic Karelian style of singing which fitted in well with Hedningarna's pungent sound. In 1992 the group made their commercial breakthrough with the CD *Kaksi!* (Two). By 1995 about 35,000 copies of *Kaksi* had

A Swedish bagpipe. Photo: Per-Ulf Allmo.

been sold, and the CD was also awarded the Swedish Gramophone Prize in the genre "Folk music and song".

Despite their orientation towards historic sound ideals, Hedningarna used electrically amplified instruments from the start,
which resulted in a musical sound and language which was
close to that of rock music. The members themselves emphasised their teenage "garage rocker" years. On the CD *Trä* (Wood)
from 1994, developments in music technology have contributed to further innovations. On one of the tunes, *Tuuli* (Wind),
Hedningarna make use of sampled material from the Swedish
Broadcasting Corporation's recordings of Sami singing (yoik),

adding fragments of "Prästpigans jojk" (The priest's maid's yoik) by Thomas Ponga (1920–57) as part of the accompaniment to the song. As an extra nicety, the Finnish Sami singer Wimme Saari (who like Thomas Ponga has roots in the North Sami village of Karesuando) takes part in the recording with a spontaneous "yoik improvisation".

Hedningarna have made use of recorded folk music material in a way that resembles the technique used by jazz musicians in *Adventures In Jazz And Folklore*. Their sources are also taken from the same archive. But the main aim is different. While the jazz musicians used the recorded material as a melodic starting point, Hedningarna use Thomas Ponga's yoik more freely, as melodic and timbral colouring. By means of computer adaptation, editing and transposition, the group has actually produced a new yoik, a fact which has also been pointed out by Sami who have heard the recording.

Hedningarna represent an important link in the development of a new phase in Swedish folk music. During the 1990s many folk music groups, both in Sweden and abroad, have made use of a "drone rock" sound which resembles Hedningarnas'.

There are several explanations for the impact of drone rock on Swedish folk music during the 1980s and 1990s. During the 1980s Swedish bagpipe music found itself at the centre of a strong "revival" movement. Courses in bagpipe-playing and bagpipe-making were organised in many parts of the country. Since the Swedish bagpipe tradition had been comatose throughout the nineteenth century, there were no models available where repertoire and performance practice were concerned, so the Swedish bagpipe revival was something of an experiment in the art of recreating a tradition. For the most part tunes were borrowed from the Swedish fiddlers' repertoire. To a certain extent, models for bagpipe technique were found in the living bagpipe tradition of other European countries, and in ensembles which specialised in medieval and Renaissance music.

The bagpipe, together with the Swedish hurdy-gurdy (which also had a "revival" of its own) and other drone instruments, revived obsolete ideals of timbre and ensemble-playing. At the same time, since the models were situated so far back in time, they allowed for considerable freedom in the combination of instruments and the style of playing. In their pursuit of historic models many folk musicians, in addition to musicians who played drone instruments, began to extend the search beyond the fiddlers' tradition. The re-entry of drone music into the Swedish folk music arena has since been manifested in special drone instrument rallies and bagpipe festivals.

At the end of the 1980s a new term was launched (not least for marketing purposes) in musical contexts—World Music. This all-embracing label was introduced by a few smaller British record companies to facilitate the sale of different types of music with various "ethnic" connections that were difficult to categorise. The term has come to mean many different things and has been used to denote all sorts of music—from local folk music forms from various music cultures throughout the world to various non-Western art music forms. On the other hand, when referring to European and North American music forms "World Music" has often come to stand for mixed music. The mixture has usually consisted of traditional folk music which has been combined with various popular music forms, such as rock, jazz, techno etc.

With the help of world music, a world-wide media-based musical arena has been created where new folk music from different cultures can be placed in what could be called a *glo-*

bal form. In this new mixed music, the rock-influenced style (illustrated by Hedningarna, for example) takes the form of a pop/rock-influenced sound, a prominent heavy "beat" accompaniment and a recording technique where the microphones are placed extremely close to the artists. Another typical feature of this style is the tendency to mix local, preferably "exotic", instruments and song techniques with this basic accompaniment. This type of music can be summed up in the combination term *global form–local content.* Hedningarna thus belongs to the same category as a multitude of "world music groups" throughout the world.

TOWARDS THE FOLK MUSIC OF THE FUTURE

It is no coincidence that Hedningarna was formed as a trio. To a far greater extent than before, 1990s' groups are made up of smaller constellations. Maybe this is a reaction to the large ensembles of the 1980s which were rather cumbersome when it came to arranging music.

More often than before, the repertoire of the folk music groups of the 1990s consists of their own compositions. Percussive and improvisational elements dominate the sound. In the improvisations (both non-metric improvisations over an underlying drone, and more melodic and rhythmic improvisations), techniques are "borrowed" from other cultures, using Greek and Turkish folk music and popular music as models, but the motifs and phrases are built up from a distinctly Swedish tonal vocabulary.

It seems as though the musical pendulum is about to swing back once again. Maybe the days of the large ensembles are over for the time being. The question is, whether drone rock has not also reached its peak in the mid-1990s. Smaller ensem-

Väsen performing at Kulturhuset in Stockholm. Photo: Per-Ulf Allmo.

bles, like Väsen, for example, with a basic combination of keyed fiddle, guitar and viola, use subtle dynamic means in their ensemble-playing, concentrating on a kind of "refined" folk music style. The group is representative of what could be called a new *chamber folk music* with intricate rhythmic patterns and finely tuned part-playing as their hallmark.

FIDDLER — ARTIST — TRADITION-BEARER

One of the twentieth century's greatest folk music idols in Sweden was the fiddler Hjort Anders Olsson (1865–1952) from the little village of Bingsjö in Dalarna in central Sweden. When Hjort Anders was "discovered" by the folk music transcriber Nils Andersson in 1907, it not only changed his situation as a musician but also his whole life. Several transcribers became extremely interested in Hjort Anders, but above all they were interested in certain parts of his repertoire.

During the first half of this century, the work of collecting folk music was based on the more or less conscious aim of illustrating distinctive local and regional features. Thus the folk music transcribers were primarily interested in Hjort Anders' older tunes with Bingsjö connections. His own compositions and his vast repertoire of tunes from the neighbouring province of Hälsingland did not attract the same amount of attention.

This interest in Hjort Anders' local Bingsjö tradition can be seen as an example of a change in attitude among the Swedish cultural élite towards the function of folk music-making. Previously the fiddlers' music had been a means, an instrument, in a social situation; a necessity at dances and ceremonies. For the transcribers, the overriding mission, both for the transcribers themselves and for folk musicians, was to perpetuate a tradition.

This view of folk music meant that greater importance was attached to local traditions, and to the "authenticity" of the fiddler. When Hjort Anders played Bingsjö tunes it was regarded as more "authentic" than when he played Hälsinge tunes, although there was virtually no difference in the learning process. Hjort Anders had learnt the tunes in his youth from other fiddlers, and from his standpoint there can hardly have been any difference between fiddlers from the province of Hälsingland and fiddlers from the province of Dalarna, as long as the tunes were good and answered their purpose as dance or concert music. In all probability it was the other way round; the Hälsinge tunes were actually more exciting and out of the ordinary for the Bingsjö audience than the "usual" local repertoire.

The rise in status of local characteristics, paired with a strong historicism, has influenced the development of fiddlers' music

Pers Hans Olsson. Photo: Per-Ulf Allmo.

during the 1900s. Musicians have stressed the importance of the locally rooted style from which the tunes have originated. Local distinctions concerning ornaments and rhythmic subtleties have been emphasised, which has led to a greater specialisation among fiddlers.

While the fiddlers' repertoire has been divided up into distinct regions during the period from the 1970s to the 1990s, it is also evident that media such as gramophone records and radio have contributed to the spread of certain types of ensemble forms, that is to say, to globalisation.

In recent times famous fiddlers such as Pål Olle (1915–87), and Pers Hans Olsson in the next generation, have not just been trend-setters within their own traditions, even if their music obviously has local roots. Their records can also be found in the record collections of nearly all of today's Swedish folk musicians. Like Pål Olle, Pers Hans comes from Östbjörka in Dalarna. He was born in 1942 into a genuine fiddlers' family. His father, Pers Erik, and his grandfather, Pers Olle, were both well-known fiddlers in the district.

Pers Hans matches up to two of the principal requirements which are demanded of today's fiddlers and tradition-bearers:

— Both his music and he himself have local roots and his music can therefore be regarded as "genuine" or authentic.

— Although Pers Hans has strong ties to the district, a large part of his repertoire consists of newly written compositions. Few of today's fiddlers have such a rich output of tunes which they have written themselves. Pers Hans can therefore be said to comply with the 1970s' and 1980s' ideal of renewal and creativity.

Besides this, Pers Hans' fiddle-playing is characterised by a highly personal expression, coupled with an excellent technique. Together with natural local roots, this helps to overcome the conflict between the demand for authenticity and the demand for innovation.

Thanks to the media, individual fiddlers, and at times particular records, have come to represent local or regional styles in folk music. Today we can point to individual fiddlers such as Pål Olle and Pers Hans as central to the Ore and Östbjörka traditions, respectively. By extension they can be regarded as symbols for the traditional fiddlers' music from the whole of the East Dalarna region, and in a wider international perspective they represent the Swedish fiddlers' tradition in its entirety. Even if their music-making starts out from older local

Lena Beronius-Jörpeland, who has twice been voted world champion keyed fiddle-player. Photo: Per-Ulf Allmo.

traditions, in many respects their personal style of expression has become a model for the development of a modern style of playing among fiddlers.

NEW INSTRUMENTAL TRADITIONS

The chromatic keyed fiddle developed during the 1920s from earlier keyed fiddle models. Eminent keyed fiddle-players from the province of Uppland played an active part in adapting the instrument to the modern folk music of those times. The modernisation of the instrument meant that it had a wider range of uses, but the keyed fiddle was to a large degree geographically limited to the region of Uppland.

In the 1960s and 1970s the keyed fiddle was the object of a newly aroused interest (similar to the renaissance that the bagpipe and hurdy-gurdy experienced during the 1980s, see above). Courses were organised in the construction and playing of the keyed fiddle. The work of collecting tunes from keyed fiddle-players who were still active was carried out by younger musicians and also by musicologists.

The most important trend-setter for the new generation of keyed fiddle-players was Eric Sahlström (1912–86). His tunes are part of almost every keyed fiddle-player's repertoire today.

Although the "keyed fiddle vogue" of the 1960s and 1970s meant that the instrument was once again spread all over Sweden and that today the instrument is also played in many other parts of the world (the States and Japan, for example), it is still primarily the players from Uppland who act as models. The female keyed fiddle-player Åsa Jinder has perhaps had the greatest impact on the mass media. On the other hand Olof Johansson in the group Väsen has played an important role as a model for other musicians in folk music circles during the 1990s.

As a consequence of increased medialisation, individual musicians and groups have come to play an even more important role as models for music-making. New types of instruments, styles and ensemble forms can now be spread in a remarkably short space of time. One of the most obvious examples is how Ale Möller, virtually single-handed, has introduced instruments that are related to the mandolin, such as the mandola, the octave mandolin, the cittern, the Irish bouzouki and even the Greek bouzouki, in Swedish folk music. He has also led the way when it comes to adapting the instruments to folk music scales by changing the positioning of the frets. Through his way of using the instruments in ensemble-playing, switching between rhythmic accompanying figures, rhythmic drones, melodies and underlying parts like a fairly free orchestral player, he has created a Swedish "bouzouki" tradition in the space of less than twenty years. This has been possible due to Möller's central role in Swedish folk music circles since the 1980s, where he has been a driving force both as a player and as a leader at numerous folk music courses. Furthermore, the impact of his bouzouki playing has been augmented by the mass media's increasing interest in folk music groups.

Similarly, other folk musicians have played a central role in the dissemination of new Swedish instrumental traditions through courses and the production of records. In the 1990s, for example, the following can be observed:

— A new percussion tradition, where "ethnic" rhythm instruments from other cultures have been adapted for use in Swedish folk music contexts.
— The development of new guitar techniques, combining part-playing and harmonic and rhythmic accompaniment.
— The revival of the bagpipe from Dalarna and the hurdy-gurdy.
— The birth of a new generation of Swedish folk music wind-players who have succeeded in making every conceivable wind instrument, from contrabass clarinets to recorders, a natural feature of Swedish folk music.

The new folk music-making has also been influenced by new educational opportunities. The Swedish adult education tradition has been an important factor in the development of folk music during the twentieth century. Thanks to the folk music vogue and the increased interest in folk music since the

1970s, folk music has been taught at innumerable courses and study groups and even at municipal music schools.

During this period folk music has also gained a foothold in higher education. Since 1976, courses in teaching methods for practising folk musicians have been available at the Royal College of Music in Stockholm. In 1995 the first senior lecturer in Swedish folk music was appointed at the same college.

NEW VOCAL TRADITIONS

Since 1970 folk song has come to have an increasingly important position in stage performances of folk music and (as in instrumental music) it is possible to name certain trend-setters in the modern folk song tradition.

Early pioneering contributions were made during the 1970s by the group Folk och rackare, who arranged songs and ballads to the accompaniment of a folk instrument ensemble. Folk och rackare can be seen as a kind of starting point for a tradition which has been confirmed during the 1990s by Lena Willemark's interpretations of ballads, for example. A comparison between Folk och rackare's LP *Stjärnhästen* (The Star Horse) from 1981, and Willemark's and Möller's CD *Nordan* (The North Wind, 1994) shows obvious similarities in tone and moods.

Nowadays it is possible to study folk song at the Royal College of Music in Stockholm. The increased interest in folk song has led to new contributions to the Swedish folk music scene, as for example folk music-singing in parts.

The folk music group Rotvälta, with Susanne Rosenberg, Sven Ahlbäck and Mikael Marin, has been one of the trend-setters during the 1980s and 1990s, not least in the field of folk song. On the CD *I Österled* (In The East) they present music from the Swedish-speaking regions of Finland. The most interesting tunes are possibly those after Alfred Lindroos (1859–1938) and Johannes Andersson (1864–1916) from the island of Stor Pellinge off the south coast of Finland. In Stor Pellinge there was a tradition of two-part folk singing from the turn of the century, a form which does not exist in any other Swedish-speaking region.

The Swedish composer Karin Rehnqvist's use of folk music, and in particular of special folk song techniques (for example *kulning*, a high-pitched form of singing used by women in the grazing pastures in the mountain regions of Dalarna), in *Davids Nimm* (1984) and *Puksånger—lockrop* (Timpanum Songs—Herding Calls, 1988), can be seen as a confirmation of the new status of folk song and of a new, sensitive way of using folk music in art music.

Considerable changes have taken place in folk music education during the last decades. Well-qualified teachers who also have a reputation as skilled performers are involved in systematic activities designed to attract young folk musicians and give them practical knowledge of style, technique and repertoire. This role of professional advisor is a new, institutionalised function in Sweden's folk music world. Through these teachers the repertoire and style of playing of Pers Hans and Eric Sahlström, for example, have been conveyed to many more musicians (and thereby more listeners) than was conceivable in earlier times.

FESTIVALISATION

When summing up the development of Swedish folk music during the latter part of the twentieth century, the first thing one notices is the new ensemble forms and instruments. European folk music groups (Irish, Greek and Hungarian, for example) together with historic ensembles, jazz bands and pop groups have influenced the development of new forms of music-making in groups.

In the fiddlers' tradition, forms of polyphony have developed, partly in the direction of a more advanced harmonic ideal with part-playing and functional harmonic accompaniment, partly towards older types of sound ideals with drones, "coarse and refined" (playing in octaves) and various types of modal harmonisations.

As a background to both group music-making and the development of the fiddlers' tradition, there is an underlying regional specialisation and historicism, alongside a situation where individual musicians more and more obviously become models for new generations.

However, the most significant changes in folk music-making concern new performing arenas. The fiddlers' competitions at the beginning of the century are a part of the transformation of folk music to concert platform music. The fact that folk music has established itself during the latter half of the century among media-based music genres has resulted in a further step in the same direction.

Over the years the fiddlers' competitions have developed into rallies and festivals, and from the 1970s onwards these festivals have become enormously important as a forum for folk music. Folk music festivals vary both in size and in form, but "festivalisation" as a phenomenon is a fairly uniform occurrence throughout the Western world.

In Sweden, for instance, the *Falun Folk Music Festival* has been organised on an annual basis since 1985. The event is marketed as an international folk music festival. At the festival in 1989, musicians from Sweden and the other Nordic countries took part, as well as musicians from Sardinia, Hungary, Estonia, Azerbaijan, Mali, the United States, the Dominican Republic, India etc, etc. The festival's 34,000 visitors could choose between 103 programme items in four days.

More than half the festival audience came from other parts of Sweden and from abroad, and had used part of their holiday to visit the festival. The majority of the visitors had also visited other festivals earlier in the summer. The major festival organisers co-ordinate their festival calendars so that both music groups and visiting audiences can take part in several festivals in succession.

The geographical and cultural medley presented at the festival was also reflected in the constellations of the individual groups. The prestigious folk music slogans of the old days—national representation, tradition and authenticity—no longer apply to festivals. Now the emphasis is on modernity, diversity and variation.

Festivalisation, concerts and medialisation are all parts of a process where the boundaries between musical genres and categories of musicians become harder and harder to distinguish. Maybe in the not too distant future we will be forced to discard the labels "folk music" and "popular music", which are already problematical. When what we today call folk music focuses less and less on reproduction and more and more on innovation, then it would seem that we have returned to the order which existed before the term folk music was first introduced at the end of the eighteenth century. Perhaps it is time to dispense with Johann Gottfried von Herder's prefix *folk* and simply talk about *music*.

A recommended record for those who are interested in following the development of Swedish folk music during the years from 1970 to 1990 is the CD box *Årsringar* (Annual Rings), MNWCD 194-195.

From 1995 to 1997 the Swedish Concert Institute, in collaboration with the Swedish Broadcasting Corporation, the Swedish Centre for Folk Song and Folk Music Research and the Royal Swedish Academy of Music, have issued a CD series on the Caprice Records label, *Folk Music In Sweden*. The series is based on remasterings of documentary recorded material and gives a comprehensive picture of the development of Swedish folk music from the 1940s to the 1990s. *Folk Music In Sweden* comprises 20 issues with a total of 25 CDs.

Another recommendation for those who want to follow the development of Swedish folk music is *Folk Net Sweden*, which is a collaboration between Swedish record producers. New folk music productions are presented via a common home site on Internet: http://www.folknetsweden.com

JAN JOHANSSON: *Adventures In Jazz And Folklore*, CAP 21475.

SKÄGGMANSLAGET: *Pjål, gnäll och ämmel* (Squeaks, Squawks and Whimpers), SLPCD-2510.

FILARFOLKET: *Vintervals* (Winter Waltz), RECD 504.

HEDNINGARNA: *Kaksi!* (Two), SRDCD 4717.

HEDNINGARNA: *Trä* (Wood), SRDCD 4721.

GARMARNA: *Guds Spelemän* (God's Musicians), MASS CD-69.

GROUPA: *Imeland*, AMCD 730.

Hjort Anders: a triple CD box with HJORT ANDERS recordings was released in 1996 by the Swedish record company Giga, GCD-22, 23, 24.

Frihetens långdans. Pers Hans Olsson spelar egna låtar (The Freedom Longdance. Pers Hans Olsson Plays His Own Tunes), GCD-13, and PERS HANS OLSSON: *Låtar inifrån* (Tunes From The Heart), GCD-37.

An interesting CD is *Till Eric* (To Eric) with compositions by ERIC SAHLSTRÖM, played by six young Swedish keyed fiddle-players, DROCD006.

ÅSA JINDER: *Trollbunden* (Spellbound) in the anthology CD box *Årsringar*, MNWCD194.

VÄSEN: *Vilda Väsen* (Wild Spirits), DROCD004.

VÄSEN: *Essence*, Ethnic B 67879.

FOLK OCH RACKARE: *Stjärnhästen* (The Star Horse), SLPCD-2691.

LENA WILLEMARK and ALE MÖLLER: *Nordan* (The North Wind), EMC 1536.

ROTVÄLTA: *I österled* (In The East), UTCD 9501.

KARIN REHNQVIST: *Davids Nimm*, PSCD 85.

Popular Music—a growing export industry

IN 1997 Sweden was declared to be the third biggest exporter of popular music in the world, second only to the United States and Great Britain. Swedish popular music is more successful than ever before, and considerably more so than the music of other comparable countries.

Twenty years ago the picture was very different. With ABBA Sweden had risen to the heights of the international pop élite, but there the group was on its own. Admittedly, a few other names had been successful abroad: Björn Skifs & Blåblus (under the name Blue Swede) had topped the USA charts with

ABBA. Photo: Lars Torndahl.

Hooked On A Feeling, Harpo had been all the rage on the continent with *Moviestar*, and in the instrumental field Bo Hansson had scored a success similar to Mike Oldfield's with the theme album *The Lord Of The Rings*.

But these were glaring exceptions in a country of provincial pop music. If the history of Swedish popular music could be divided into neat, ten-year chapters, then the 1960s was the decade when we learnt to imitate English pop music and the 1970s was the decade when we struck out on our own and tried to develop a distinctive, Swedish pop tradition.

Now that we have reached the 1990s this has given us a double advantage. Swedish pop music is characterised by a well-developed ability to assimilate foreign styles, combined with an identity of its own—which, paradoxically, is often difficult for Swedes themselves to identify.

THE ERA OF THE "PROGRESSIVE" MUSIC MOVEMENT
Basically, the provincial character had two sources. Firstly, for many decades there had been a popular hit culture with old roots, symbolised by the Swedish top-of-the-pops charts, "Svensktoppen". Secondly, from the end of the 1960s there had been a politically-based alternative culture, the so-called "progressive" music movement, which pursued the idea of a decentralised, non-élitist, non-commercial music culture from a left-wing perspective.

During the 1970s, largely due to this music movement, Swedish pop music was divided into two camps. You were either part of the music movement or you were against it—ideologically correct or not correct, "progressive" or commercial. To take up a position outside these camps was no easy matter.

ABBA, by definition, was commercial, and therefore controversial in their native country. At the same time they were reaping a rich harvest throughout the world. The music movement's position was so strong that a large proportion of the pop music that was produced during the 1980s must be viewed as a reaction to, or as an extension of, the movement. And its effects are still noticeable.

Sweden's biggest independent record company, MNV, for instance, is one of the music movement's flagships—even if nowadays its musical profile is not appreciably different from other companies. Among other things, in recent years MNV was the first company to sell Swedish pop music to Asia: Japan, Korea, China and other countries. Punk is another example, which first appeared towards the end of the 1970s. Initially, the music movement wanted nothing to do with the punks, since their political analysis was so primitive—bordering on non-existent. However this attitude was soon reversed; the aggressiveness of punk was interpreted as a healthy reaction to an unjust society. Today the progressive music movement's most obvious heirs are to be found in the punk movement (there is even such a thing as "prog" punk in Sweden) with an emphasis on non-élitism, Swedish lyrics and meaningful content, often with political undertones. Dia Psalma, Köttgrottorna and De Lyckliga Kompisarna are examples of such punk groups.

During the 1960s all Swedish pop groups sang in English. During the 1970s, on the other hand, it was almost a provocation to do so. This attitude lingered on into the 1980s, long after the music movement had lost its dominating role. As a rule, both hit chart groups and alternative groups sang in Swedish. The so-called "neo-romanticism" in Great Britain had Swedish imitators such as Lustans Lakejer and Ratata, and post-punk was represented by such names as Reeperbahn, Brända Barn and Imperiet, all of whom sang in Swedish. The same was true of several of the popular hit chart groups—Gyllene Tider, Noice, Magnum Bonum, Freestyle, Factory and Snowstorm—even, oddly enough, those that had English names.

Another trend during the 1970s and 1980s consisted of what may be called ballad rock or troubadour rock, a counterpart to the singer/songwriters in the States. Names such as Ulf Lundell, Ola Magnell, Dan Hylander and Magnus Lindberg may have leant towards foreign models—not least Bob Dylan—but the language was Swedish and the literary/poetic ambition was high.

HIP HOP AND HARD ROCK—THE EXPORT SUCCESSES OF THE 1980S

However, only in exceptional cases have Swedish lyrics attracted overseas listeners. In the beginning of the 1980s Sweden produced yet another international hit group, the English-speaking Secret Service, which on the continent and in South America in particular scored hit after hit, including *Oh Susie*, *Ye Si Ca* and *Flash In The Night*.

Hard rock had never felt comfortable with the Swedish language either, even if attempts had been made. In the mid-1980s Sweden suddenly produced two international stars in this category. The first was guitarist Yngwie Malmsteen, who moved to America at the beginning of the 1980s and joined the American groups Steeler and Alcatrazz. Yngwie Malmsteen then set up on his own and became an international superstar, with all the international superstar's mannerisms. The second was the soft metal group Europe from Upplands Väsby (a suburban town north of Stockholm), who made their breakthrough in Sweden in 1982 when they won the Swedish Rock Championship. Their international breakthrough came in 1986 with the single *The Final Countdown* on the album with the same name, whose success they have never managed to repeat, however.

Both Europe and Yngwie Malmsteen also attracted attention at an early stage in Japan, where Swedish hard rock soon built up a faithful audience. During the 1980s there was a steady flow of hard rock groups that were exported to Japan—Treat, Biscaya, Heavy Load, Torch, Madison—many of whom were more successful in Japan than back home in Sweden. This encouragement helped to make Swedish hard rock a genre which attracted a remarkably large number of musicians. During the 1970s there was very little in the way of hard rock in Sweden; by the end of the 1980s one could easily get the impression that half of Sweden's rock musicians played hard rock. From time to time a group—Candlemass, for instance, or Electric Boys—even succeeded in reaching beyond the special audience of hard rock fans, but mostly it was the sheer number of groups that was impressive.

At the beginning of the 1990s Sweden also came to be a leading name in the more extreme form of hard rock called death metal, with groups such as Entombed, Dismember, Unleashed and Grave. The number of groups in this field was also amazingly large. Internationally, Sweden ranked as death metal country No. 2 after the United States. Entombed could sell 200,000 copies of a record on the international market, even if everything was still underground.

GARAGE ROCK THEN AND NOW

Another English-speaking trend also became noticeable in the mid-1980s, namely so-called "garage rock"—a name which referred to ferocious and primitive rock music which was recorded in restricted circumstances in the 1960s, primarily in the United States, and which attained an increasingly strong cult status during the 1970s and after the punk era.

The Nomads, a group from Solna on the northern outskirts of Stockholm, was the first Swedish group to make a name for itself in garage rock, which spread rapidly through the international underground scene. Soon it had developed into a whole movement, with groups such as Shoutless, Bangsters, Bottle-Ups and Backdoor Men.

During the second half of the 1990s there has been an unexpected sequel to this trend: a whole series of groups has emerged with roots in the old Detroit groups Stooges and MC5, and also, in a figurative sense, in the Swedish group Union Carbide Productions which kept the tradition alive in the late 1980s and early 1990s. Now The Hellacopters have kick-ass-rocked their way to national fame; Silverbullit, Cry, Mother Superior, Mazarine Street and Chunks are following in their tracks. In addition, half of Union Carbide Productions has been reincarnated in The Soundtrack of Our Lives, which with the privilege of seniority perpetuates the same tradition with unexpected refinement. A rock form which a few years ago seemed outworn and depopulated has been reborn—young and vital.

THE NEW DANCE MUSIC

Towards the end of the 1980s the international wave of new dance music began to make itself felt. The first artist to win real success was Leila K together with Rob'n'Raz, whose *Got To Get* climbed most of the European hit charts during 1989 and 1990. This was followed by two Swedish rappers, Papa Dee and Dr. Alban, and two female singers, Kayo and Titiyo. Under the name "Nordik Beat" attempts were made to launch

The Hellacopters.
Photo: Lars Torndahl.

the new Swedish dance music as a united movement—with only a certain measure of success.

A couple of years later it seemed as though there was hardly any modern Swedish dance music being produced that wasn't exported to at least one or more country: Army of Lovers, Melodie MC, Pandora, Legacy of Sound, Leila K, Basic Element, Clubland, Stakka Bo. However, a few years into the 1990s all previous records were broken by Ace of Base, a quartet from Gothenburg who, despite the boom in Swedish dance music, had had to turn to a Danish record company for a record contract.

Hits such as *The Sign* and *Happy Nation* were like a plague that swept over country after country—not least Sweden. The debut album *Happy Nation* (*The Sign* in America) came to be the world's most sold debut album ever, selling twenty-two million copies. The follow-up album, *The Bridge*, didn't come anywhere near these figures, however, and was therefore considered a flop, despite sales of over six million copies.

All this went on in English. Meanwhile, in their native country, Swedish artists with a wider repertoire continued to sing in Swedish: Magnus Uggla, Eva Dahlgren, Ulf Lundell, Marie Fredriksson, Pugh Rogefeldt, Peter LeMarc, Monica Törnell, Björn Afzelius, Dan Hylander and Robert Broberg.

Towards the end of the 1980s new names were also established, such as Orup, Freda', Thomas Di Leva, Tommy Nilsson, Suzzies Orkester and Mauro Scocco, followed in the 1990s among others by Anders Glenmark, Niklas Strömstedt, Lisa Nilsson, Staffan Hellstrand, the sisters Irma and Idde Schultz, Lisa Ekdahl, Cajsa Stina Åkerström and Bo Kaspers Orkester. The list could be considerably longer.

This kind of broader artist seldom sings in English. Mikael Rickfors is a rare example, but his popularity also rocketed when he switched to Swedish on the record *Vingar* (Wings) in 1988. Tomas Ledin is an even more obvious example. During the 1970s he became one of Sweden's best-loved artists, not least with the last-dance-type ballad *I natt är jag din* (Tonight I Am Yours). In the early 1980s he switched to English in his songs and was soon marginalised as an artist. In 1990 he made his come-back, in Swedish, and quickly became even bigger than before.

In all fairness, the case of Lolita Pop can admittedly be used to prove the opposite. Throughout the whole of the 1980s the group struggled on as post-punkers with a limited audience. Towards the end of the 1980s they made a serious attempt to break through in America; they switched to English for the song lyrics, with the surprising result that absolutely nothing happened in America, but they made their breakthrough on a wide front at home in Sweden.

Certain people then placed Lolita Pop in what was known

Thomas Di Leva.
Photo: Lars Torndahl.

as "the ten-year quota", an ironic term which was introduced to describe how certain groups that had been in existence quite a while and had had a small cult following, suddenly found themselves to be widely established. The same thing happened to Eldkvarn, Docenterna and Wilmer X during the latter half of the 1980s.

One English-speaking exception was Roxette, which was created by Per Gessle together with the singer Marie Fredriksson. Per Gessle was already an established hit-maker in Swedish with the group Gyllene Tider (whose success during the first years of the 1980s was later surprisingly surpassed during a temporary reunion in 1995 and 1996). At first Roxette appeared to be an affair with a broad, but purely Swedish, appeal. Then followed one of the most romantic success stories imaginable; an American exchange student bought Roxette's second LP in Sweden in 1988, took it back home to Minneapolis and persuaded the local radio station to play it. Listeners were so enthusiastic that the record was issued there as well, which was the beginning of a triumphal procession which established Roxette both in Europe and the USA, as well as in South America, Australia and Asia.

SWEDISH INDIE POP

Otherwise, much of Swedish pop music's success in recent years is founded on what is known as the "indie pop wave". Originally indie (an abbreviation of independent) was just a term for music from small, independent, record companies, as distinct from the large companies. However, by the beginning of the 1990s it had become a genre in its own right. People talked about indie pop, by which they meant a kind of pop music with big bad guitars and sweet little pop melodies, with a strong underlying energy and dreamy, disembodied singing. In Sweden the group Easy was the first to make a name for itself. There were many small groups already in existence, admittedly, but this quartet from Gothenburg managed to get a record contract with the English record company Blast First, the same record label which one of the forerunners of the genre, American Sonic Youth, had issued records on.

A launching campaign ensued in the press, but Easy never really broke through, neither in Sweden nor abroad. But they did open a door, which Popsicle would just walk through soon afterwards. This was a group of four young men from Piteå in the north of Sweden who had moved to Stockholm. They knew the new pop music like the back of their hand and interpreted it tastefully and becomingly, besides which they did it on Telegram, one of Sweden's hippest record companies. After Popsicle it was as though a bung had been pulled out. Suddenly Sweden was swamped with young, modern, ambitious pop groups: This Perfect Day, The Wannadies, Eggstone, Brainpool, Steve-

Popsicle. Photo: Lars Torndahl.

pops, Suredo, Happydeadmen, Blithe, The Bear Quartet, Muf-
flon 5 and others.

FIRST JAPAN—THEN THE WORLD

Part of this vogue eventually found its way to Japan, where a
Swedish pop trend emerged during 1994 and 1995. The forerunners were Eggstone and The Wannadies, but it was The
Cardigans who really caught on. In the spring of 1995 *Carnival*
with The Cardigans was a huge hit in Japan. The group became megastars; both the producer Tore Johansson and the
studio Tambourine in Malmö were surrounded by a veritable
cult, and Japanese fans rapidly adopted group after group after
group: Cloudberry Jam, Pinko Pinko, The Excuse, Leslies,
Scents, Cinnamon, Confusions, Ray Wonder. Only on rare

occasions had these groups made any noise at all in Sweden.

And soon the female singers arrived on the scene. Names such as Meja, Jennifer Brown, Sophie Zelmani, Dede, Mayomi, Fatima Rainey and Pandora have also been successfully launched on a wide front. Meja and Jennifer Brown now rank among the biggest international artists in Japan. In 1996 Meja's debut album was the most purchased foreign record in Japan, with a sale of about 800,000 copies. Meanwhile things have also been happening in other places during the 1990s. Whale, for instance, a temporary project with three all-round artists involved in music and media in Stockholm, put together an unpretentious hard rock funk tune complete with video, *Hobo Humpin' Slobo Babe*, which soon became an unexpected international hit, not least in America.

Other Swedish groups that attracted attention in the States were Salt and Souls, who were both a little too raw in tone for the Japanese fans. Hard rock rapping Clawfinger had substantial successes in Germany and Great Britain, among other countries. In 1996 the group Fireside from the north of Sweden landed a contract with the legendary Rick Rubin's company, American Recordings, and the same year the group toured throughout the States with the Lollapalooza Festival, an alternative rock festival which assumed cult proportions and which has been called the Woodstock of the 1990s. The following year the female grunge group Drain was given a similar position in Ozzy Osbourne's touring whole-day festival Ozzfest. During 1996 The Wannadies and The Cardigans began to attract attention in Britain, and The Cardigans also began to cause a stir in the States. Both groups have added fuel to the Swedish pop wonder, which the media in both America and Britain are beginning to write about more and more. And increasingly The Cardigans are beginning to look like Sweden's world-wide pop group success No. 5, after ABBA, Europe, Roxette and Ace of Base.

SWEDISH SOUL, R&B AND HIP HOP

And maybe name No. 6 is already on the way. At the time of writing (autumn 1997), teenage singer Robyn has been climbing the American charts for the last months, and so far no-one can say where it will all end. Her success is also a sign of a new, prevailing trend in Swedish 90s' pop, namely soul—or R&B as the genre's modern variety is often called. It is a relatively recent phenomenon, even if the closely related dance music has been going strong for nearly a decade.

Artists like Titiyo, Mauro Scocco, Lisa Nilsson and Eric Gadd can be regarded as forerunners of this genre. In the case of Eric Gadd the year 1997 witnessed his definite breakthrough as a broad popular artist, although he sings sophisticated soul music in English. And the flood of recording artists continues unabated: Jennifer Brown, Stephen Simmonds, Blacknuss All-stars, André de Lange, Dilba, Arnthor, Lutricia McNeal, George Cole, Fatima Rainey, Dede, Sadie, Mayomi—all soul-based artists who only a few years earlier would have been regarded as exclusive, verging on the unsellable on the Swedish market.

The story of Swedish hip hop is a similar tale. For a long time it was an almost invisible genre. The first group to appear was the fun-loving, dyed-in-the-wool Swedish group Just D. The Latin Kings from the Stockholm suburb of Alby had a different profile. This was a group of second generation immigrants whose rap lyrics were peppered with suburban slang. And here again it was as though a cork had been pulled out. Three years after The Latin Kings' debut the list of Swedish hip

The Latin Kings. Photo: Ulf Berglund/Pressens Bild.

hop names is almost endless. Infinite Mass, Sherlock, Absent Minded, Boogaloo, Addis Black Widow/Bus 75, Goldmine, Bechir, Brigade and Ro-Cee are some of the more notable groups.

None of the groups rap in Swedish, however, although both Just D and Latin Kings did. This is symptomatic —the Swedish language is out of favour in the Swedish pop world today, which is a little strange, considering that it is easier for artists that sing in Swedish to sell more records in Sweden. It is as though the focus is automatically on the international market, even though the chances of succeeding there must presumably be much smaller.

JAZZ, POP AND FOLK ROCK

Another 1990s' trend consists of female jazz singers bordering on pop, or if you prefer, female pop singers with jazz backgrounds. Rebecka Törnqvist was the first name to appear, a trained jazz singer who sang sophisticated, jazzy pop, accompanied by young jazz musicians. She caught on in a big way in Sweden and has now also made a name for herself in France.

She was followed by a succession of singers: Viktoria Tolstoy, Sara Isaksson, Lina Nyberg, Jeanette Lindström. The most special name, without any doubt, is Stina Nordenstam, even if the epithet "jazz singer" was only used at the beginning of her career. Three records later she has gone through a rare and unexpected development, from a sort of jazz-influenced art pop in Rickie Lee Jones style to a ragged, impressionistic and highly individual music which has caused a considerable stir in international circles—above all among artists and musicians. It has also led to a big demand for her voice, which has been featured on records with such cult names as American Anton Fier and the Swiss group Yello.

As a sort of counterweight to international styles, Swedish folk rock has also taken on a new lease of life in recent years, a music form which was hardly breathing during the 1980s (see chapter "Folk Music"). An important part has been played here by Hedningarna, a trio of distinguished folk musicians who have widened the boundaries of Swedish folk music in at least two ways during the 1990s: firstly, they have experimented with

Kent. Photo: Lars Torndahl.

sampling, distortion and other techniques in a way which no Swedish folk group had ever attempted before, and secondly, they have unexpectedly added two female Finnish singers to the group, whose style of singing comes from an archaic tradition from eastern Finland, while the rest of the group has continued in the Swedish folk tradition.

Their success was immediate, and they were suddenly joined by a large number of Swedish folk rock groups, such as Garmarna, Hoven Droven, Big Fish, Vadå and Den Fule. The biggest group of all, however, was Nordman, a project involving the *Riksspelman* (National Folk Musician) Mats Wester and the hard rock singer Håkan Hemlin which caught on with an extremely uncommon force. So far the group's two records have sold over 900,000 copies in Sweden alone, even though irate critics are of the opinion that the music and lyrics possibly convey a hidden chauvinistic message.

So the Swedish language has not been completely wiped out in Swedish pop music. And even in the most modern pop there are exceptions, for example bob hund, one of Sweden's most obstinately original groups with an electric, resolute music and surrealistic lyrics in the Skåne dialect from southern Sweden.

More significant probably is the success of the group Kent, a group from Eskilstuna who play modern rock from the indie culture—heavy but sensitive, with poetic lyrics by the charismatic singer Joakim Berg. Success was not long in coming; presumably it was greater and more immediate than if the group had sung in English. Successful imitators have already appeared in the form of the two groups Jumper and Scott.

The problem, of course, is that Kent can hardly be exported in its present state. And when Sweden's export is so successful it's hard not to dream of other countries. But it still seems to be easier to be successful in Sweden if the song lyrics are in Swedish.

DISCOGRAPHY

ABBA: *Arrival* (1976), POLYDOR 533981-2.
The record that established ABBA as international superstars. Includes *Dancing Queen*.

GYLLENE TIDER (1980), 7942192 (Parlophone).
Sweden's most popular pop group at the beginning of the 1980s. Later on the singer Per Gessle formed Roxette. In 1996 a reunion tour was made, and the group's popularity grew even greater.

ULF LUNDELL: *Kär och galen* (A Fool For Love, 1982), SWEETHEART CDP7 463102.
Has been called Sweden's Dylan as well as Sweden's Springsteen. The song *Öppna landskap* (Open Landscapes) has been suggested as Sweden's new national anthem.

THE NOMADS: *Where The Wolf Bane Blooms* (1983).
The record that started the Swedish garage rock trend. The Nomads became an international cult group, the first Swedish rock group to break through in the toughest rock music field.

IMPERIET: *Blå himlen blues* (Blue Heavens Blues, 1985), MLRCD 45.
Sweden's leading rock group in the 1980s, with a production which sometimes has a little 1980s' stiffness about it but with several tunes which have become Swedish classics.

EUROPE: *The Final Countdown* (1986), 4663282.
Sweden's biggest hard rock export, introduced by a fanfare which has been adopted by brass bands and cocktail pianists alike.

ORUP (1988), 2292-44708-2 (1989) (ORUP - 2).
Bright pop music in a lighter style with witty lyrics. Thomas "Orup" Eriksson had a whole row of flops behind him; today he is one of Sweden's most established artists.

ROXETTE: *Look Sharp!* (1988), 7910982 (Parlophone).
Breakthrough album for two artists who were already established in their own right in Sweden. *The Look* is the title of the hit tune which was the beginning of Roxette's international career.

ROB 'N' RAZ featuring LEILA K (1990).
The single *Got To Get* launched Swedish dance music on the road to success. Still today Leila K is one of Sweden's most colourful and most controversial artists.

EVA DAHLGREN: *En blekt blondins hjärta* (A Bleached Blond's Heart, 1991), STATCD 29.
Sweden's most respected female artist. Her most successful record was also her last pop record for a long time.

HEDNINGARNA: *Kaksi!* (Two, 1992), SRSCD 4717.
Swedish folk music as it has never sounded before, with fuzzed-up Swedish lute and two female Finnish singers. Paved the way for a new folk rock trend.

POPSICLE: *Lacquer* (1992), TCD-19 4509-92211-2.
The group that started the Swedish indie pop trend, with characteristically sweet pop tunes and hard guitar sound.

ACE OF BASE: *Happy Nation/The Sign* (1992).
The most sold debut album in the world, released on a Danish record label after a large number of Swedish record companies had refused it.

REBECKA TÖRNQVIST: *A Night Like This* (1993), EMI 8277862.
The first name in a long succession of young female Swedish singers somewhere between jazz and pop. Several of them were in the same class at the Royal College of Music in Stockholm.

NORDMAN (1994), SLPCD 2866/521 771-2 (SONET).
A keyed fiddle-player and a hard rock singer combined forces and produced Sweden's most sold record in the 1990s—and also one of the most controversial records.

THE LATIN KINGS. *Välkommen till förorten* (Welcome To The Suburb, 1994), EW (East West) 4509-96250-2.
Sweden's first genuine hip hop in Swedish, with angular production and lyrics which divided Sweden in two camps.

BOB HUND (1994): *Silence,* SRSCD 4720 (1993).
Sweden's most out-of-the-way rock. Five determined young men and a singer bursting with energy, with surrealistic lyrics in the Skåne dialect and a completely new approach to the branch.

THE WANNADIES: *Be A Girl* (1994), SNAP 16.
Swedish indie pop with even sweeter tunes than Popsicle and the others. Popular in England, although trouble with a record company nearly put a stop to their introduction there.

84

KENT (1995), RZA/BMG 74321 26507 2.
The group that made Swedish a modern rock language again. High tension rock with indie background and ambitious, poetic lyrics.

FIRESIDE: *Do Not Tailgate* (1995), STAR 416-2.
Swedish hard pop bordering on hard core, adopted by Rick Rubin's American Recordings. Asked to play at the American Lollapalooza festival.

ROBYN: *Robyn Is Here* (1995), 74321 31835 2.
Blond Swedish teenager who sings soul music in English. Made her breakthrough in Sweden and then took America by storm, although Americans regard her as a pop-singer.

THE CARDIGANS: *First Group On The Moon* (1996), 533 117-2.
The third record in a three-stage rocket to the international pop heights. With the help of the hit *Lovefool* they conquered both the United States and Europe. Japan had already been won.

STINA NORDENSTAM: *Dynamite* (1996), 0630-18240-2 (Telegram Records Stockholm).
Began as a jazz singer, was described as a Rickie Lee Jones imitation. By her third record she had developed into Sweden's most artistically radical singer, with a world-wide reputation to boot.

THE SOUNDTRACK OF OUR LIVES: *Welcome To The Infant Freebase* (1996), 0630-16652-2 (Telegram Records Stockholm).
Swedish psychedelic rock in cinemascope format. A new group of rock veterans from Gothenburg who made an immediate breakthrough.

ERIC GADD: *The Right Way* (1997), STM 50042.
Soul with both 1990s' and 1970's sound. A breakthrough on a broad front from a veteran who helped turn Swedish musical taste from white to black.

Jazz in Sweden—a contemporary overview

WHAT MAKES Swedish jazz so Swedish? What does it have that Belgian, French, English ... or American jazz lacks? A hunt for distinctive national elements in Swedish jazz yields little in the way of answers. One musician who immediately springs to mind, of course, is baritone saxophonist Lars Gullin (1928–76), whose folkloristic and romantic music definitely fits the description; during the 1950s disparaging voices even referred to it as "*fäbodjazz*" (goatherd's jazz). However, Gullin's music is more a reflection of his own personality and of the scope that jazz allows for individualism in general, rather than a typical expression of the specific qualities that characterise Swedish jazz.

Nevertheless, the music is sometimes said to have a character of its own which non-Swedish musicians and critics from time to time have tried to define: a sparse, lyrical quality, often in combination with a typically Nordic melancholy that is sometimes thought to be an expression of our climate—the dark, cold winters and the long, light summer evenings—and of the Swedish scenery, with its deep forests and high mountains. These qualities are not only restricted to the jazz versions of Nordic and Swedish folk tunes that were introduced in the 1960s by pianist Jan Johansson (1931–68) and others, an artistic method of working which Swedish jazz musicians have made use of from time to time and which has experienced a revival in the World Music era of the 1990s.

However, what above all distinguishes Swedish jazz from that of other countries is its historical background, rather than the character of the music itself. During the last sixty years or so it has attained a remarkably high artistic standard, stimulated by domestic as well as external influences and experiences. Swedish jazz of the late 1990s has tremendous breadth and variety, encompassing top quality representatives of many styles—from ragtime and New Orleans jazz to fusion experiments and free improvisation, unfettered by formal boundaries.

LOUIS LIT THE FLAME

One could perhaps say that jazz came to Sweden on Wednesday the 25th October, 1933. That was the day that Louis Armstrong gave his first concert in Stockholm, before a large, youthful audience that was completely captivated by his playing.

The interest in Louis Armstrong turned out to be far greater that anyone had reckoned on. The organisers had only planned one concert, but the demand was overwhelming and in next to no time the tickets had all been sold. Three more concerts were hastily arranged—and still the audience kept coming. On the Saturday evening something highly unusual occurred: Sweden's only radio channel rescheduled its programmes so as to be able to transmit part of Louis Armstrong's concert live. In a way this was an acknowledgement of the greatness of Louis Armstrong's music. Moreover, it was not an isolated event, an exotic and irreverent manifestation in Swedish musical life. Nor was it a one-off, commercial concession to the increasingly barbaric taste of the young. Louis Armstrong signalled the beginning of a new age, the start of the first musical revolt among young people. Even the newspaper critics could not stem the tide with their supercilious and prejudiced comments—"music from a madhouse" and "ape language from the jungle" and other similarly exaggerated epithets.

For many people, Armstrong's concerts in Sweden (six in all) were a decisive turning point. The audiences included many musicians who would be responsible for creating the Swedish jazz of the 1930s and 1940s. They have borne witness, fervently and convincingly, to the positive shock they experienced—to the intensity of Armstrong's trumpet playing, and his powerful presence on the concert platform, so completely different from anything that had ever been seen or heard in Sweden before.

Some of them, such as trumpeters Gösta Törner (1912–82) and Thore Ehrling (1912–94), were in their twenties and had already begun to establish a name for themselves as jazz musicians. Gösta Törner was to become the first jazz soloist of stature, while Thore Ehrling became the most successful big band leader in Sweden during the swing era. Others, still very young, were not to emerge until much later. One of these was trumpeter Rolf Ericson (1922–97) who at the age of eleven was taken to the concert by his uncle.

Of course there had been jazz in Sweden before this, but Armstrong's visit marked the climax of a long period of development, like a birth at the end of a long pregnancy. And it was not just the music itself; the event also broke with traditional patterns. Previously Sweden's cultural influences had mainly come from Germany and Central Europe. From now onwards the younger generation would look to the West for inspiration.

As early as the mid-1920s young Swedish musicians had begun to take an interest in the new sounds from America. Early visits to England by The Original Dixieland Jazz Band and other musicians from America were reflected in the playing of British musicians who appeared at fashionable venues in the Swedish capital. Many young Swedish dance band musicians were highly impressed by the standard of their playing. Some of these Swedish musicians (who subsequently formed The Paramount Orchestra) worked their way to New York, playing on an ocean liner, and there they were able to experience Jean Goldkette's band and other famous constellations in the flesh. Jazz-influenced orchestras also gave guest performances in Sweden. From the end of the 1920s there are examples on Swedish records of dance tunes and popular songs that are liberally spiced with improvised solos.

However, it was after the Armstrong concerts that interest in jazz really blossomed and developed into a youth movement. In November, 1933, the first number of *Orkester Journalen* (OJ for short) was published—today *Orkester Journalen* is the oldest jazz magazine in the world. Soon a young generation of musicians was producing expert improvisers who not only showed stylistic sensitivity but whose playing was also personal and imaginative.

By this time American gramophone records had become their main source of inspiration. British dance bands could also be heard on radio transmissions from London in the evenings. On the other hand, the Swedish Broadcasting Corporation's attitude to jazz continued to be decidedly niggardly until well into the 1940s. Isolated concerts with guest artists from America (Coleman Hawkins in 1935, Benny Carter in 1936,

Jimmie Lunceford in 1937, Edgar Hayes and "Fats" Waller in 1938 and Duke Ellington in 1939, to mention a few legendary names) acquired tremendous importance and were often something of a milestone in the development of Swedish musicians. In 1939 concerts by Django Reinhardt and Stephane Grappelli (Quintette du Hot Club de France) had a decisive impact on several young instrumentalists, some of whom even formed their own "Swedish Hot Quintet".

From the start Swedish jazz was a reflection of American models. But even if American styles were imported wholesale, Swedish jazz had its own distinctive profiles. The first genuine jazz records were produced in the mid-1930s, and in 1936 the Sonora record company began to record outstanding Swedish jazz musicians in small groups, led by bassist Thore Jederby (1913–84). These sessions were issued on a series of records under the band name Swing Swingers. They constitute a unique document of Swedish jazz in the 1930s and also of the skilled jazz soloists who in everyday life disappeared in the anonymity of the big dance bands and light orchestras, where they had little scope to display their talents.

SWING IT, PROFESSOR!

By the outbreak of World War II the American swing fever was under way in earnest in Sweden. The latest idol was an immensely popular teenage singer called Alice Babs (b. 1924), who made a resounding breakthrough in 1940 with her singing in *Swing it, magistern* (Swing it, Professor!), a film set in a school where the jazz music was like a breath of fresh air compared to the stuffy, old-fashioned music education. However, representatives of the music establishment and other conservative forces were incensed. Alice Babs was accused of being a bad influence and even of posing a serious threat to the younger generation. Alice Babs worked and recorded with Duke Ellington on several occasions from the early 1960s onwards, and she was even appointed *hovsångerska* (Singer to the Royal Court of Sweden).

During the war years Sweden was isolated from the rest of the world, and the import of jazz records and guest artists was effectively cut off. At the same time the entertainment business was blossoming and the demand for music was greater than ever. All this meant that Swedish jazz expanded rapidly. Jazz was played at dance venues all over the country, by orchestras large and small and by amateurs and professionals. The music of the young generation also had a considerable impact on radio and film. Furthermore, the lack of imported records resulted in a drastic increase in the number of domestic recordings.

Inspiration still came from America, however. Isolated records which found their way over the Atlantic with convoys or which were circulated in other ways, worked like a vitamin injection. Short wave transmissions were picked up, first from England and later on from the areas of Europe that were occupied by the allied troops. Some young musicians even sat by their radios with pen and paper, transcribing melodies and arrangements so as to pick up the very latest ideas from America.

During this period a new jazz generation was emerging in Sweden. It included many soloists with highly personal styles, such as clarinettists Åke Hasselgård (1922–48) and Putte Wickman (b. 1924), trumpeter Rolf Ericson, alto saxophonist Arne Domnérus (b. 1924) and tenor saxophonists Carl-Henrik Norin (1920–67) and Gösta Theselius (1922–76), to name but a few.

Rolf Ericson with Charlie Parker 1950. © *Orkester Journalen.*

OPEN BORDERS

Understandably, there were many musicians who nurtured dreams of travelling to the homeland of jazz, which became possible once the war was over. Two of these were Hasselgård and Ericson, who both went to America in 1947. "Stan Hasselgård", as he was called in America, rapidly became a well-known name, even making his own recordings in the United States. He was also featured as soloist in Benny Goodman's septet and led his own band on 52nd Street in New York until his untimely death in a car crash, only 26 years old. Rolf Ericson played in several well-known bands, including those of Woody Herman and Charlie Barnet (and later on with Stan Kenton, Duke Ellington, Charles Mingus and others). This—the very fact that Swedish jazzmen could make an impact "over there"—drastically altered the perspectives of those who remained at home.

Post-war jazz in Sweden was in fact of very high quality. Unexposed to the ravages of war, the music had been able to develop freely, and Sweden's isolation had merely been beneficial. The end of the war also meant that the flow of records and guest artists from America was resumed, bringing with them new impulses. Early in 1948 Dizzy Gillespie and his legendary bebop big band toured Sweden for two weeks. The following year saxophonist James Moody made some of his most successful recordings (including "Moody's Mood for Love") with local musicians in Stockholm, and in 1950 Charlie Parker toured Scandinavia with a Swedish band. Two young American saxophonists—representatives of the budding "cool" style—were to have an even stronger influence on Swedish jazz; Stan Getz and Lee Konitz both toured Sweden in 1951, and Getz recorded *Ack Värmeland du sköna* (later entitled "Dear old Stockholm") with a quartet that included 18-year-old pianist Bengt Hallberg (b. 1932). This venture—the first time that a Swedish folk tune was blended with the language of jazz—was a huge success, not only in Sweden but also in the United States.

A number of Swedish soloists now came to the fore, each with a distinctive and personal profile: Hallberg, Domnérus, Wickman, Gullin and trombonist Åke Persson (1932–75), to mention the most successful.

A SWEDISH "STAR"

Lars Gullin was the most significant personality in Swedish jazz of the 1950s, and one of the very few independent jazz voices to emerge in Europe. His warm, sensitive sound on the baritone sax and the smooth flow of his playing, his imaginative improvisations and inventive arrangements and composi-

Lars Gullin 1956. Photo: Bengt H Malmqvist.

tions with their characteristically beautiful melodies and moods—all this put Lars Gullin in a class of his own. He was more widely acclaimed in international circles than any other Swedish musician of the decade.

In 1954 Gullin made a successful tour in Great Britain, and the same year he was voted top "New Star" on his instrument in Down Beat's international critics' poll—without ever having visited the United States. Gullin's recordings were released in America, however, and in many other countries as well, as was other Swedish jazz music. The Swedish record companies also took the opportunity to record visiting American musicians together with their Swedish colleagues. Gullin was on many of these recordings—with Moody, Getz, Zoot Sims, Clifford Brown and others.

To a large extent jazz was still music that people danced to, and it appealed mainly to the younger generation. For the most part it was played by small or middle-sized groups, but there was one big band which also made its mark on the Swedish jazz scene: Harry Arnold's Swedish Radio Studio Orchestra. Formed in 1956, the band provided a variety of dance music, pop music accompaniments and jazz for broadcasts on a part-time basis. Its members consisted of leading Swedish jazz soloists, many of whom fronted their own groups. Being a skilled and versatile leader who frequently worked in film and recording studios, Harry Arnold (1920–71) wrote most of the repertoire himself. However, he also welcomed contributions from guests, one of whom was Quincy Jones, who recorded a highly acclaimed album with the orchestra in 1958.

The 1950s witnessed the dawn of a more artistic attitude towards jazz-playing, but the increasing complexity of the music, although applauded by many critics and "serious" jazz listeners, frequently led to conflicts with agents and dance enthusiasts. By the beginning of the 1960s a new generation of jazz musicians was ready to take over. They were mainly inspired by the new black jazz from America, represented by names such as Coltrane, Rollins, Mingus, Blakey and Miles Davis. However, the young Swedes suddenly found themselves in a no-man's-land: rock 'n' roll and pop were now the music of the day, jazz was no longer suitable for dancing to, and the commercial entertainment industry lost interest in it. At the same time, jazz found itself shunned by the cultural establishment and cut off from its subsidies.

Thus the 1960s were hard times, both socially and economically, for jazz in Sweden. The only American-type jazz club which survived any length of time was Gyllene Cirkeln (The Golden Circle) in Stockholm, which opened in 1962 and featured both American guests and Swedish bands, but its policy gradually changed in favour of other musical genres. Jazz venues in other larger cities, such as Gothenburg and Malmö, were short-lived, while in other parts of Sweden jazz events were rare or non-existent.

Musically, however, the 1960s was a strong decade. Tenor saxophonist Bernt Rosengren (b. 1937), who led his own groups, stood out as a leading force, one of the first young Swedish soloists to emulate the language of American hard bop, albeit with a distinctly personal style of playing. Rosengren became a rich source of inspiration for many of his contemporaries, not only musically but also morally, since he insisted on playing his own music despite the tough times that Swedish jazz was going through. His music eventually developed towards greater improvisational freedom under the influence of American cornet-player Don Cherry, who worked in Sweden for long periods. Don Cherry also played an important part in integrating folk music material with jazz. In the early 1970s Rosengren was part of the group Sevda, playing jazz improvisations on Turkish folk melodies in uneven rhythms such as 7/8 and 9/8. Sevda was led by the Turkish trumpeter Maffy Falay (b. 1930), who has lived in Sweden since the 1960s. Later on Rosengren returned to his musical roots, playing bebop-based music and even fronting his own big band at concerts and dance venues.

Trombonist Eje Thelin (1938–90), who toured throughout Europe with his quintet, also played an important role. His

Bernt Rosengren.
Photo: Christer Landergren.

playing was strongly influenced by Miles Davis although (like Rosengren's) it had a strong personal identity of its own. Thelin became disillusioned with the Swedish jazz scene and moved to Austria, where he taught at the conservatory in Graz for several years. He also performed free improvised music with his own groups in several European countries. In 1972 he returned to Stockholm, however, and formed a group which became one of the leading exponents of jazz in Sweden throughout the decade. Later on Thelin mainly devoted his energies to composing and to performing as a soloist. Eventually the music of both Rosengren and Thelin developed towards free improvisation, but each returned to his musical roots during the 1970s.

Alto saxophonist Christer Boustedt (1939–86), who played the leading role in the widely acclaimed movie "Sven Klang's Quintet" in 1976, and pianist Lasse Werner (1934–92) combined bebop-based jazz with theatrical effects. Trumpeter Lars Färnlöf (1942–94) and his quintet, which he shared with pianist Staffan Abeleen (b. 1940), developed a somewhat lyrical version of the American hard bop style, based on Färnlöf's excellent compositions, many of which featured rhythms and melodic lines which had an affinity with Sweden's musical heritage. *Grandfather's waltz* became widely known, for instance, and was recorded by Stan Getz and other artists.

Singer Monica Zetterlund (b. 1937) attracted attention abroad, recording with American pianist Bill Evans and appearing in America, England and other countries. She still pursues an active career as a jazz singer and at the same time has developed a parallel career as a highly acclaimed film star and stage show artist.

JAZZ IN SWEDISH

Arne Domnérus had formed an orchestra in 1951 which played at the Nalen dance palace in Stockholm for more than a decade and also at dance venues all over the country. When jazz no longer functioned as dance music, Domnérus and his musicians began to look for new combinations and new platforms for their artistry: churches and concert halls, collaboration with chamber music players, symphony orchestras and choirs and so on. They also made up the core of the Radio Jazz Group (formed in 1967 as a successor to Harry Arnold's big band) which for many years was led by Domnérus.

An important role in this development was played by the pianist Jan Johansson, who extended the boundaries of jazz and attracted new audiences with his sensitive interpretations of Swedish folk tunes, *Jazz på svenska* (Jazz in Swedish). In a way, this was a development of the "Swedish-sounding" jazz

*Putte Wickman and Arne Domnérus. Photo: Nilla Domnérus/
Orkester Journalen.*

music created by Lars Gullin some years earlier, but here it was
not just a matter of seeking inspiration in Swedish music—
Johansson went straight to the source, the Swedish folk melodies themselves, and interpreted them in his own highly personal way.

Other jazz composers, such as bassist Georg Riedel (b. 1934),
trumpeter Bengt-Arne Wallin (b. 1926) and pianist Bengt Hallberg, also broadened their repertoire and made forays into this
field. These experiments reflected a new attitude, not just
among Swedes but among European jazz musicians in general. Instead of just trying to sound American they now focused on their own musical heritage.

A pioneer in this area was pianist and composer Nils Lindberg (b. 1933). Lindberg, who grew up in the district of Dalarna
and came from a family which had strong connections with
folk music, had been playing and composing jazz with an un-

99

mistakable (although initially unintentional) Swedish flavour for ten years or more. Lindberg, who was associated with such jazz musicians as Gullin, alto saxophonist Rolf Billberg (1930–66) and trumpeter Jan Allan (b. 1934), proved his worth in the 1960s with a couple of widely acclaimed albums.

It was not easy for Swedish jazz to gain respect and support from the cultural establishment. When demands for grants to jazz musicians were first expressed in the early 1960s, one daily paper described the idea as "unrealistic", while another stated that "such money would go directly to public bars and be spent in a few days."

A couple more anecdotes may serve to illustrate general attitudes towards jazz in Sweden during this period. In 1962 Nils Lindberg was commissioned by Swedish Television to write a large-scale piece of music for symphony orchestra and jazz soloists to be broadcast over the whole of Europe. When he called his work "Symphony No. 1", the protests from the Society of Swedish Composers were so vociferous that he was forced to rename the piece more modestly as a "concerto". Pianist Gugge Hedrenius (b. 1938) encountered resistance from the opposite direction; since the early 1960s he had fronted his own "Big Blues Band", with many excellent jazz soloists among its members. In the mid-1960s a dance restaurant in Stockholm terminated the orchestra's contract prematurely on the grounds that Hedrenius and his musicians were playing jazz. The spectacular legal proceedings that followed ruled in Hedrenius' favour: music with improvised solos *can* be used for dancing.

Hedrenius still maintains his musical profile in the late 1990s, playing for ballroom audiences that "listen with their entire bodies", as he puts it. Lindberg is still widely respected for his concert music as well as his jazz works—and the two are often integrated.

Changes in Swedish cultural policy eventually eased the situation for jazz. Following a parliamentary resolution in 1974, jazz was one of several new genres to receive governmental support in the form of annual grants to music groups and eventually also to concert arrangers. The Swedish Jazz Federation *(SJR)* which was formed in 1948 had more or less become an organisation for record-collectors by the 1960s. Now, however, it re-emerged as a network of jazz societies, which have gradually increased in number. At the present time there are more than a hundred jazz societies throughout the country, most of which arrange public concerts on a regular basis, some more frequently than others. Some also hold annual festivals, the oldest and best-established being the Umeå International Jazz Festival (founded in 1968) in October, and the Kristianstad Jazz Festival (founded in 1971) which is held in July.

The 1970s also saw the evolution of municipal music schools throughout the country that offer every child, starting from third grade, the chance to learn a musical instrument. These schools have stimulated and broadened musical life in Sweden. They offer tuition in a large variety of musical instruments and genres, including big band music, rock and jazz. Parallel with this development the Swedish Concert Institute regularly arranged concerts at schools all over the country, thus introducing jazz and other musical genres to young people. By the late 1970s jazz had also become a recognised subject at the Royal College of Music in Stockholm and other higher education institutions. After many years of waning interest all this meant a welcome regeneration of both jazz musicians and listeners.

The common interests of jazz musicians were manifested in

several more or less short-lived organisations that were formed from the mid-1960s onwards, primarily in Stockholm and Gothenburg. After many years of arranging concerts at different venues, the Stockholm-based Federation of Swedish Jazz Musicians *(FSJ)* eventually received municipal and governmental support in 1977 to take over the club Fasching at Kungsgatan 63 in the centre of the Swedish capital. Since then this former discothèque has been a centre for jazz, presenting both Swedish and international attractions. At about the same time the club Nefertiti was established in Gothenburg. Although there are equivalents in several other cities, only Fasching and Nefertiti operate on a full-time, professional basis, with a programme policy that reaches beyond the sphere of jazz (also embracing rock, blues, World Music and various forms of dance music), whereas other local jazz concert organisations around Sweden depend on voluntary work by jazz enthusiasts.

After the early 1960s very few gramophone recordings of Swedish jazz were produced. However, early in the 1970s, the Swedish Concert Institute started to present jazz on its subsidised record label Caprice Records, producing one or two jazz albums a year. In the early 1980s the government began to support independent record companies that focused on jazz and other non-commercial types of music, and this support has drastically changed the situation. Since 1954, the jazz magazine *Orkester Journalen* has given an annual Golden Disc award to the best Swedish jazz record of the year, selected by its readers and a jury of critics. In 1968 the poll had to be cancelled, since hardly any Swedish jazz records were issued that year. By the late 1980s about fifty Swedish jazz albums were being released each year, a figure that has since been doubled (*Orkester Journalen* calculated that the estimated playing time of the output on records of Swedish jazz in 1995 was equal to the entire output of the period 1954–69!). This increase in jazz recordings is not only the result of financial support but is also due to the fact that the number of jazz musicians and groups on a professional level has been doubled and re-doubled several times during the past twenty-five years. Moreover, technical development has provided wider access to professional recording equipment. The advent of the compact disc in the 1980s made the overall production process easier to handle. Most Swedish jazz albums are released by small companies, several of which are owned by musicians.

MODERN MAINSTREAM

From the 1970s onwards many different forms of jazz have led parallel (and in some cases integrated) lives in Sweden. The scene has been dominated by what could be described as "modern mainstream", based on the jazz of the 1950s and 1960s. One reason for this is that jazz education has generally emphasised the formal rules of the musical language and repertoire of that era. Another reason is that this tradition has been passed on by the still very active 1960s' generation to young, up-and-coming players. The boundaries of this style have also been widened, allowing for a greater amount of freedom. Nowadays almost anything is possible, from the very formal to a free, intuitive exchange of musical ideas. The ever-expanding repertoire not only encompasses a wealth of new compositions but also material derived from ethnic sources and other non-conventional contexts.

Pianist Bobo Stenson (b. 1944) and bassist Palle Danielsson (b. 1946) were among the rare young musicians of the 1960s who chose to make jazz their means of expression. Both gained wide musical experience early on, working with leading Swedish musicians as well as American guest artists. The two joined forces in the quartet Rena Rama, one of the most influential Swedish jazz groups of the 1970s. The repertoire mostly consisted of compositions by members of the quartet, as well as folk music material from Africa and Asia. Together with another member of Rena Rama, saxophonist Lennart Åberg (b. 1942), Stenson also worked with Turkish drummer Okay Temiz's group Oriental Wind. As the name suggests, Oriental Wind focused on musical material from Turkey, the Middle East and India. In the 1970s Stenson also had a quartet of his own together with Norwegian saxophonist Jan Garbarek, who in his turn worked with Palle Danielsson in American pianist Keith Jarrett's widely acclaimed quartet. With his brilliant, imaginative bass playing, Danielsson has enhanced concerts and recordings in numerous countries during the 1990s, both with his own group and in collaboration with many top names in jazz. Bobo Stenson has been a member of American saxophonist Charles Lloyd's quartet for many years. He also plays in numerous Swedish groups, but his most notable success has been as leader of his own trio with bassist Anders Jormin and Norwegian drummer Jon Christensen. The music is sparse and dynamic with a sensitive interplay between the three musicians. Jormin (b. 1957) is a brilliant and imaginative instrumentalist who has also fronted several groups of his own. He has recorded a remarkable solo album and written music for a variety of settings and contexts, including theatre plays.

Pianist Lars Sjösten (b. 1941), who is also a prolific composer, has been at the forefront of Swedish jazz for 35 years, working and recording with numerous American jazz soloists and leading his own bands, from trios to octets. In his own personal way Sjösten has continued along the musical path mapped out by Lars Gullin, with whom he often collaborated. Gullin's son Peter (b. 1959) has intrepidly taken up the baritone saxophone, his late father's instrument. Peter Gullin also plays other saxophones and is a composer and soloist in his own right. He performs with his own trio and has written music for a variety of ensembles, including chamber groups, choirs, symphony orchestras, solo piano and big band. One of the first jazz musicians in Sweden to derive inspiration from India and the Orient was pianist Jan Wallgren (1935–96), who played "raga-based" jazz in the 1960s. Later on Wallgren composed chamber music, solo pieces, songs and even an opera, while still keeping up his jazz activities. He was an inspiration and mentor to many, an artist who refused to accept stylistic boundaries.

American bassist Red Mitchell (1927–92), who lived in Stockholm from 1968, played a significant role on the Swedish jazz scene, fronting groups of his own and often working with American jazz soloists on their visits to Europe. From the start Mitchell collaborated with many leading Swedish soloists: trumpeter Bosse Broberg (b. 1937) and tenor saxophonist Nils Sandström (b. 1942), both of whom belonged to the 1960s generation, played in his group Communication in the 1970s, and later on Mitchell also collaborated with younger players, in particular saxophonist Joakim Milder (b. 1965), who stands out as one of the strongest and most independent voices in Swedish jazz of the 1990s. Milder's expressive resources range from chamber music to pop. As a soloist on tenor and soprano sax his playing is sparse, contemplative and immediately recognisable.

Milder is one of many young players who began their careers in the band led by drummer Fredrik Norén (b. 1941).

Since 1978 Norén has fronted an ever-changing, hard bop-based quintet that has included several young musicians who have later come to the fore as leading exponents of jazz. One is tenor saxophonist Tomas Franck (b. 1958), who has lived in Copenhagen for many years and is a featured soloist in the Danish Radio Big Band.

Trumpeter Anders Bergcrantz (b. 1961) from Malmö has also played with many Danish groups in Copenhagen as well as fronting bands of his own; his American quartet has appeared at famous jazz venues in New York City. Alto and soprano saxophonist Håkan Broström (b. 1955) is not only a noted soloist and leader of his own group but also an excellent composer. Numerous younger musicians, such as trumpeter Peter Asplund (b. 1969) and alto saxophonist Johan Hörlén (b. 1967) play music in the wide field of modern mainstream. Pianist Jan Lundgren (b. 1966) has collaborated with several musicians from previous generations, most notably Arne Domnérus. The main part of his wide range of activities consists of a trio with bass and drums which plays music firmly rooted in jazz tradition, while at the same time making successful explorations into material that is significantly Swedish, ranging from folklore to pop music.

Pianist Åke Johansson (b. 1937) is one of many musicians from the older generation who maintain the musical language of their younger years. He is a member of the group CBQ (Contemporary Bebop Quintet), which also includes tenor saxophonist Stefan Isaksson (b. 1956). One of the foremost soloists in this style, tenor saxophonist Krister Andersson (b. 1951), is also one of the most frequently recorded. He began his musical career as a clarinettist in the classical field, appearing as a soloist and in chamber music groups, and he still uses the clarinet occasionally in jazz contexts. Another well-known soloist is baritone saxophonist Gunnar Bergsten (b. 1945), who is featured with several groups as well as fronting his own quartet.

Trumpeter Gustavo Bergalli (b. 1940) from Argentina and saxophonist Hector Bingert (b. 1944) from Uruguay are two of many immigrants who have made their mark on the Swedish jazz scene. Bergalli is a noted soloist in the hard bop tradition and he has also combined tango and jazz. Bingert fronts his own group, Latin Lover, and in recent years he has also had his own big band. He has played jazz which is strongly influenced by candombé and other Latin-American styles. American pianist Steve Dobrogosz (b. 1956) is another "jazz immigrant" whose artistic range encompasses choral and chamber music as well as pop music. He has perhaps been most successful as the writer of lyrics and songs, which he has performed and recorded (mostly in duo settings) with singer Berit Andersson (b. 1953) and others. Since 1954 Norwegian drummer Egil Johansen (b. 1934) has lived in Sweden, working in many of the leading jazz ensembles of this country and also fronting his own bands.

"FREE" AND "HAPPY"

In the 1970s Swedish musicians were strongly influenced by "free jazz" (without formal boundaries) and "fusion" (jazz with rock rhythms and electronic instruments). As in other European countries, "free" jazz musicians didn't derive their language primarily from American jazz but from a vast number of sources, including folk music of different ethnic origins, rock music, contemporary art music and electronic music, to name but a few.

Iskra, formed around 1970 by players from different backgrounds (including drummer Sune Spångberg (b. 1930), who had belonged to the new hard bop generation of the 1950s) and active until the early 1990s, became a pioneering force in this area, both as a concert group and as leaders of musical workshops in schools, hospitals and other institutions. Lokomotiv Konkret, founded in 1977, is fronted by saxophonist Dror Feiler (b. 1951) who also has an established name as a composer of art music. In recent years saxophonist Mats Gustafsson (b. 1964) has been the leading Swedish exponent of freely improvised music in Sweden, working in many different combinations on the international scene. For most musicians, however, the element of free improvisation has been incorporated into the different formal structures of modern mainstream, in particular by pianist Per Henrik Wallin (b. 1946). Wallin's compositions and arrangements (mostly played by a trio but occasionally by larger ensembles) combine jazz ingredients with a multitude of other components while at the same time offering opportunities for all kinds of spontaneous expression. Brus Trio, with pianist Anne Forsén (b. 1960), bassist Ulf Åkerhielm (b. 1962) and drummer Gilbert Matthews (b. 1943), a South African expatriate, has specialised in free jazz as well as playing original compositions, folk music-influenced arrangements and jazz standards.

One of the first Swedish bands to fuse jazz and rock (and occasionally African and Latin-American music as well) was Egba, led by trumpeter Ulf Adåker (b. 1945) and saxophonist Ulf Andersson (b. 1940), two musicians with roots in the jazz of the 1960s. Several other musicians of that era also expanded their vocabulary to include the electronic sounds of the day, collaborating with younger musicians whose background was mainly in rock. One of the latter is pianist and keyboard-player

Harald Svensson (b. 1954), who has also been involved in other groups, most notably Entra. Tenor saxophonist Ove Johansson (b. 1936) and keyboard-player Susanna Lindeborg (b. 1952) in the group Mwendo Dawa have combined acoustic instruments with electronic sounds since the 1970s, and there are several other groups which work with fusion types of jazz. Lars Jansson (b. 1951) began on the organ and electric keyboards but later concentrated on acoustic piano. His trio, with drummer Anders Kjellberg (b. 1952) and bassist Lars Danielsson (b. 1958), mostly plays Jansson's own compositions. The subtle, intimate interplay between the musicians and the consistently high standard of the trio make it one of the most interesting jazz groups in Sweden. Danielsson, who also has a background in fusion and pop, is another of Sweden's internationally renowned bass-players. He is involved in several international groups and also fronts his own multi-national combinations.

Entra and several of the other groups mentioned above are based on the west coast of Sweden and have strong connections with the musical scene in Gothenburg, a city that is also the home of many excellent jazz musicians. The saxophone group Position Alpha (formed in the early 1980s) has remained one of the most original and creative ensembles, experimenting with different settings and means of expression, including theatrical effects. One of its leading members, alto saxophonist Thomas Jäderlund (b. 1958), also plays an important role in Änglaspel, a band which was formed in 1977. Änglaspel is led by pianist/composer Stefan Forssén (b. 1943) and covers a wide musical spectrum, from march-like tunes through bebop-style material to sentimental songs.

There is a strong tradition of guitarists in Swedish jazz. The dean of this cadre is Rune Gustafsson (b. 1933), a master instrumentalist and versatile, melodic soloist who worked in Arne Domnérus' group for many years. Gustafsson has also made a number of albums under his own name which have been circulated abroad. Two other excellent guitarists are Göran Klinghagen (b. 1955), with his sensitive sound and melodic phrasing, and Max Schultz (b. 1960), whose range varies from sparse lyricism on the acoustic guitar to the energetic electricity associated with rock. Internationally, the most famous Swedish jazz guitarist of the 1990s is Ulf Wakenius (b. 1958), who has worked and recorded with many megastars, including pianist Oscar Peterson. He also leads his own Swedish group, playing a type of music that fits neatly into the fusion category.

Sweden had its share of the Dixieland and New Orleans revival movements in the late 1940s, and has had a vast number of traditional groups ever since. In the early years most of these orchestras were made up of college students. In recent years, however, there have also been quite a few professional groups working in this area, and several have even gained international fame. Kustbandet, founded in the early 1960s, re-creates the music of the early big band era (Henderson, Ellington etc) and has toured world-wide. One of its members, trumpeter Bent Persson (b. 1947), is widely acclaimed and takes part in events throughout the world, often in an all-star line-up modestly called The Swedish Jazz Kings.

With the opening of the jazz pub Stampen (The Pawnshop) in the Old Town of Stockholm in the late 1960s, Sweden also experienced a renaissance of swing music. A sign over the stage saying "Happy jazz, please" gave the music a new label. Clarinettist Ove Lind (1926–91) was in the forefront of this movement, performing music in the style of Benny Goodman's small groups. One of his co-musicians, vibraphonist Lars Erstrand

Ulf Wakenius with Ray Brown. Photo: Christer Landergren.

(b. 1936), has later fronted his own unit and has appeared as guest soloist with bands all over Europe.

Sweden also witnessed a big band revival, mainly in the form of amateur orchestras with older musicians or connected to music schools. It was estimated that Sweden had about 400 big bands in the mid-1970s and quite a few have survived to the present day. Some have risen to a semi-professional level, such as the Sandviken Big Band, founded in 1968 in the small town of Sandviken. From 1971 and onwards the twenty-five or so military bands in Sweden have been transformed into regional music institutions with a wide range of commitments. Norrbotten Big Band (based in Luleå) and Bohuslän Big Band (based in Uddevalla) are two examples of such bands which have developed into large jazz orchestras, working more or less on a full-time basis together with different composers and guest soloists. Stockholm has several big bands with some of the foremost jazz soloists in their ranks; trombonist Mikael Råberg (b. 1959) and trumpeter Bosse Broberg lead two of them, playing their own compositions and arrangements, while trumpeter Fredrik Norén (b. 1957) is the initiator of the Stockholm Jazz Orchestra which has collaborated with several famous American composers and soloists at concerts and recordings. Saxophonist and composer Helge Albin (b. 1941) heads the Tolvan Big Band in Malmö which plays a repertoire of pieces which have mostly come from his own pen. In the same town saxophonist Jörgen Nilsson (b. 1948) fronts the Monday Night Big Band which plays music by (or in the tradition of) the late American composer/arranger Thad Jones. The band performs once a week at a local pub and also tours occasionally.

TRADITION AND RENEWAL

Although the regeneration of players has its counterpart in a regeneration of listeners, jazz remains a rather exclusive genre. However, a more open attitude to jazz at music colleges in recent times has meant that young musicians now have greater freedom of choice. Thus there are several performers whose artistry encompasses jazz, folk music, rock, pop and other forms of expression with apparent ease. Many of the young, college-trained jazz musicians also come from very diverse backgrounds, which is sometimes reflected in their work.

The emergence of World Music has put a popularity stamp on experiments that have been going on in jazz for a very long time. Many musicians have continued to merge jazz and folk music in the 1990s, although with a wider scope of material (from Asia, Africa and the Orient as well as from the Nordic countries). A pioneer in this area is percussionist Bengt Berger (b. 1942), who studied in India and Africa in the 1960s and 1970s. He has been the initiator of numerous groups working with music from various ethnical backgrounds, some very obscure, such as West-African funeral music (The Bitter Funeral Beer Band). Another veteran is Roland Keijser (b. 1944), a saxophonist (and player of many other flutes and reed instruments) whose roots are in bebop music but who early on extended his musical language into other fields. One of his 1990s' projects is Marrakesh wedding music, which he performs enrobed in a caftan with a fez on his head. Saxophonist Jonas Knutsson (b. 1965) plays in a diversity of styles, including fusion and experimental rock, but has been particularly acclaimed for his work in the Swedish folk music tradition. Knutsson plays soprano sax with folk music fiddlers, and he has also been involved in several World Music projects, including pianist Elise Einarsdotter's (b. 1955) ensemble which specialises in jazz with a strong folk music flavour. He has also played in groups with singer Lena Willemark (b. 1960) and multi-instrumentalist Ale Möller (b. 1955), both of whom are primarily folk musicians but who also have a love of the language of jazz and readily use it in their music-making. Pianist Esbjörn Svensson (b. 1964) plays in a conventional jazz trio with bassist Dan Berglund (b. 1963) and drummer Magnus Öström (b. 1965), but the scope of the trio has been extended by way of media exposure and appearances at rock festivals and other non-jazz venues. With their backgrounds in rock and pop, Svensson, Berglund and Öström also relate easily to other forms of African-American music and collaborate successfully with artists from these and other areas. Another versatile musician is trombonist (and sometimes singer) Nils Landgren (b. 1956), whose most notable suc-

Esbjörn Svensson Trio 1998. Photo: Nilla Westin/Ordagrann.

cess has been in the musical styles known as "soul" and "funk" Pianist Anders Widmark (b. 1963), who occasionally appears as a singer, has also explored these and other areas; one of his latest projects in which he played old Swedish psalms in a jazz trio setting attracted considerable attention in 1997. Other brilliant jazz pianists with a wider musical range include Jacob Karlzon (b. 1970) and Anders Persson (b. 1958), both of whom mainly work with their own trios (with bass and drums) as well as appearing in numerous other musical settings.

"Cross-over" artists in Swedish jazz include a couple of veteran singers. Svante Thuresson (b. 1937) started out as a jazz drummer in the 1950s and since then has ventured into various different areas of pop music while still retaining his love for jazz and leading a quartet that includes pianist Gösta Rundqvist (b. 1945). Claes Janson (b. 1947), who started out as a hootenanny singer in the 1960s, is a well-known and popular jazz and blues performer who works with several bands, including Öhman's Organ Grinders, led by Hammond organist (and pianist) Kjell Öhman (b. 1943).

Several female singers, in particular Viktoria Tolstoy (b. 1974) and Rebecka Törnkvist (b. 1964), have also made a name for themselves in the pop music sphere, thus drawing wider attention to their jazz performances. Others, such as Lina Nyberg (b. 1970) and Jeanette Lindström (b. 1971), have preferred to concentrate on jazz. Both lead their own groups and perform their own songs—a reflection of the development in jazz education which has resulted in a higher status for singers in the jazz community (both Nyberg and Lindström have studied at music college, in company with several other young jazz artists).

There are a number of young instrumentalists who work with their own groups and perform their own repertoire, such as saxophonists Per "Texas" Johansson (b. 1969), Fredrik Ljungkvist (b. 1969), Magnus Lindgren (b. 1974), Jerker Lindström (b. 1966) and Fredrik Carlquist (b. 1969). They are all highly skilled musicians who have been through music college, yet each has his own distinctive voice. The strong individuality of each of these players (and many others) firmly refutes the criticism that has been expressed from time to time that the music education results in musical conformity, with "mass-produced" players who are all cast in the same mould.

SUBSIDISED BY MUSICIANS

Unfortunately, the fervour of the modern Swedish jazz scene is not matched by a similar interest from the media or from a larger audience. In spite of state support to musicians and concert arrangers alike, Swedish jazz still struggles under the cold star of hardship. Few musicians can earn a decent living purely by playing jazz: out of the large number that try, very few attain anything more than a very modest material standard.

In practice, prevailing conditions mean that it is the jazz musicians themselves who are the biggest and most important supporters of this form of music. In comparison with the Royal Opera in Stockholm, where every ticket is state-subsidised to the tune of considerable sums (about 90 percent of the actual cost), every ticket to a jazz event is subsidised by the musicians, who rarely (if ever) manage to earn a reasonable income from their work.

As in other European countries, jazz musicians find it difficult to compete with American stars and groups who dominate the major festivals as well as the production of record albums.

However, there is a strong sense of self-esteem and a high level of artistic morale in Swedish jazz, two important factors in maintaining a high class of musical performance, even by international standards.

There are CDs available, in some cases several, with practically every band or artist mentioned in the chapter.

The early development of jazz in Sweden can best be followed in a series of CDs published by Caprice Records, the record label of the Swedish Concert Institute. "The History of Swedish Jazz" (*Svensk jazzhistoria*) consists, so far, of five volumes (each with two CDs), all of which are accompanied by booklets with a wealth of information (each has an English summary) and illustrations:

Vol 1 *Jazz Warning* (1899-1930) CAP 22037.
Vol 2 *The "Hot" Epoch* (1931-36) CAP 22038.
Vol 3 *Rhythm & Swing* (1937-39) CAP 22039.
Vol 4 *Wartime Swing* (1940-42) CAP 22040.
Vol 5 *"Jazz attacks"* (1943-47) CAP 22026.

A continuation of this series is under way.

Swedish Artists—a selection

THE PRINCIPLES for this selection of artists have been that they have an established international name and that their recordings are relatively easy to find in the shops. These recordings can be found on a number of different record labels and most of them are also mentioned in the discography of Swedish composers.

SINGERS

Swedish singers have always held a strong position in international circles. Ever since "the Swedish nightingale" Jenny Lind (1820–87), Sweden's perhaps most famous artist of all time, started out on her short but intense international career in 1843, the Swedish Voice has been a recognised concept. Jenny Lind left the opera stage in 1849, however, and began to sing oratorio and Lieder. From 1860 to 1887 the soprano Christine Nilsson (1843–1921) took over where Jenny Lind left off and enjoyed extraordinary success in Paris, London, Russia and America. Unfortunately, no recordings of either Jenny Lind or Christine Nilsson have been preserved.

In more recent times Elisabeth Söderström has held a unique position among lyric sopranos. After innumerable appearances at the Royal Opera in Stockholm between 1950 and 1980, combined with an extensive international career, she was appointed director of the Drottningholm Court Theatre from 1993 to 1996, the same theatre where she made her début in 1947. Other notable lyric sopranos include the versatile Margareta Hallin,

Helena Döse, MariAnne Häggander, Britt-Marie Aruhn, Iwa Sörenson, Laila Andersson Palme, the English soprano Rosemary Hardy who mainly focuses on the contemporary repertoire, Lena Nordin, Hillevi Martinpelto, Christina Högman and Katarina Dalayman.

Wagnerian sopranos who have appeared on opera stages throughout the world include Birgit Nilsson, Berit Lindholm and Catarina Ligendza, all of whom have now reached the end of their active singing careers, as well as Siv Wennberg. One of their most famous predecessors who celebrated triumphs in Bayreuth and at the Metropolitan was Nanny Larsén-Todsen (1884–1982), while the contralto Karin Branzell (1891–1974) and the mezzo-soprano Kerstin Thorborg (1896–1970) were leading interpreters of the big Wagner roles. The versatile contralto Kerstin Meyer has been acclaimed for her interpretations of both the older and the more modern repertoire in Berlin and Hamburg and at Covent Garden and Glyndebourne. Many prominent opera artists have emerged over the last 30–40 years, including the contralto Barbro Ericson and the mezzo-sopranos Margot Rödin and Sylvia Lindenstrand. Birgitta Svendén appears on opera stages throughout the world and the same is true of Anne Sofie von Otter, who has achieved world-wide acclaim and has also won several prizes for her sensitive and personal Lieder interpretations.

The names of Jussi Björling (1911–60), Nicolai Gedda and Gösta Winbergh shine especially brightly among the list of Swedish tenors. Older Wagner tenors include Set Svanholm (1904–64) who was also director of the Royal Opera in Stockholm from 1956 to 1963 and Helge Brilioth. Their predecessors, all of whom appeared frequently on records, include Martin Öhman (1887–1967), Oscar Ralf (1881–1964) and

Torsten Ralf (1901–54), while Claes-Håkan Ahnsjö, who mainly performs in Germany, and Stefan Dahlberg are two of their most recent successors.

Legendary baritones include John Forsell (1857–1941) who was the powerful director of the Royal Opera from 1924 to 1939, Sigurd Björling (1907–83) and Joel Berglund (1903–85) who was director of the Royal Opera from 1949 to 1956. For many years the all-rounder Erik Saedén was one of the mainstays of the Royal Opera and was also an influential singing teacher. Ingvar Wixell, who for many years has been attached to the Deutsche Oper in Berlin, Håkan Hagegård, Jerker Arvidson, Carl Johan Falkman and Krister St. Hill are all active in the international field. The cadre of versatile younger artists includes Mikael Samuelson, whose congenial Bellman interpretations have been highly appreciated, Olle Persson and Peter Mattei. Notable Swedish basses include Bengt Rundgren, who is based in Germany and who continues the tradition after the legendary Sven Nilsson (1898–1970).

INSTRUMENTALISTS

Pianists are well represented among Swedish instrumentalists and many of them are well-known in international circles. Hans Leygraf has worked abroad for many years (mainly in Salzburg), both as a concert pianist and—like so many other successful soloists when they begin to reach the end of their active soloist careers—as a teacher. Greta Erikson has also played a significant role, both as a soloist and as a teacher. The middle generation includes such names as Carl-Axel Dominique, the Hungarian pianist Janos Solyom, the Catalan pianist José Ribera, the Italian pianist Lucia Negro, all of whom live and work in Sweden, as well as Olof Höjer, Marian Migdal, and

Dag Achatz who is based in Switzerland. In addition Staffan Scheja and his younger colleagues Roland Pöntinen, Love Derwinger, Anders Kilström, Mats Widlund, Bengt Forsberg, Hans Pålsson and Bengt-Åke Lundin perform both in Sweden and abroad. Peter Jablonski has made a sensational international career, both as a concert pianist and on record.

Indefatigable champions of contemporary music include Mats Persson and the German pianist Kristine Scholz, while Jan Eyron and Lars Roos have played important roles as accompanists.

Prominent organists include Alf Linder (1907–83), Erik Lundkvist, Ralph Gustafsson and Hans Fagius, who has appeared extensively on record. Karl-Erik Welin (1934-92) and Hans-Ola Ericson also have established reputations as composers, while Gunnar Idenstam has also made a name for himself as a brilliant improviser.

Notable guitarists include Göran Söllscher, Per-Olof Johnson, Per Skareng and Mats Bergström. Magnus Andersson mainly focuses on contemporary music while Jakob Lindberg has devoted his attentions to the lute and the performance of early music.

The trombone-player Christian Lindberg and the trumpeter Håkan Hardenberger have both built up world-wide reputations as virtuosos on their instruments, both in the classical and in the contemporary repertoire. Both are richly represented on record.

Clas Pehrson and Dan Laurin are two well-known recorder-players who concentrate on early music. Notable oboists include Alf Nilsson and the versatile Helén Jahren who has given the first performances of numerous works which have been written especially for her. Notable clarinettists include Håkan Rosengren, Kjell-Inge Stevensson, Kjell Fagéus and two new young stars: Martin Fröst and Karin Dornbusch. The bassoon-player Knut Sönstevold, the horn-player Ib Lanzky-Otto and the tuba-player Michael Lind are all top-ranking Swedish instrumentalists.

Leading string players include Leo Berlin, Karl-Ove Mannberg, Mats Zetterqvist, Nils-Erik Sparf, Bernt Lysell, Tobias Ringborg, Per Enoksson, Anna Lindal and Ulf Wallin. Notable cellists include Frans Helmerson, Torleif Thedéen, Mats Rondin and Chrichan Larsson, who is also a composer.

CONDUCTORS

Prominent Swedish conductors on record include the legendary opera conductor and Björling accompanist Nils Grevillius (1893–1970), Tor Mann (1894–1974), who was responsible for raising the standard of Swedish orchestras, the uncompromising principal opera conductor Sixten Ehrling, who for long periods has also worked in Detroit and New York, Stig Westerberg, who has an extensive knowledge of the repertoire and who has been an indefatigable champion of new works, Ulf Björlin (1933–93), Johan Arnell who works in Germany, and the opera conductors Kjell Ingebretsen from Norway and Thomas Schuback. Herbert Blomstedt conducted the Swedish Radio Symphony Orchestra between 1977 and 1982 and the Dresdner Staatskapelle between 1975 and 1985, after which he was appointed principal conductor of the San Francisco Symphony Orchestra. Since 1996 he has been employed by the Norddeutscher Rundfunk in Hamburg. With his focus on period instruments, Arnold Östman made a pioneering and well-documented contribution to the 18th century repertoire during his period as director of the Drottningholm Court Theatre. Notable younger conductors who have begun to attract attention include Cecilia Rydinger Alin and Niklas Willén.

Eric Ericson has a unique position among choral conductors, both in Sweden and abroad. Other well-known choral conductors include Dan-Olof Stenlund, Anders Öhrwall, Anders Eby, Gustaf Sjökvist and Stefan Parkman.

STRING QUARTETS

Notable string quartets include the Kyndel Quartet, the Fresk Quartet and the Saulesco Quartet, all of which are now dissolved, while the Zetterqvist Quartet, the Yggdrasil Quartet (which for many years was attached to the University of Aberdeen), the Lysell Quartet and the Tale Quartet are among the most successful Swedish quartets in international circles in recent times. The Stockholm Arts Trio should not be forgotten in this context.

CHAMBER ORCHESTRAS

Prominent chamber orchestras include the Stockholm Chamber Orchestra *(SNYKO),* the Stockholm Sinfonietta and the Swedish Chamber Orchestra which is based in Örebro. The KammarensembleN and Sonanza focus particularly on contemporary music.

During the summer months concerts are given by the Stockholm Ensemble (artistic director Mats Liljefors), and the National Museum Chamber Orchestra, which was formed by the cellist and conductor Claude Génetay (1917–92) for the museum's concert series and which nowadays is conducted by Thomas Schuback. Musica Vitae in Växjö and Camerata Roman in Oskarshamn are other notable chamber orchestras.

OTHER ENSEMBLES

The Drottningholm Baroque Ensemble (founded in 1971) and the Westra Aros Pijpare from Västerås perform the Baroque and Renaissance repertoire on period instruments. Since 1978 the percussion ensemble Kroumata has had a faithful and enthusiastic audience throughout the world and has made a large number of highly acclaimed recordings. The Stockholm Saxophone Quartet has made a name for itself by giving first performances of newly commissioned works. Another ensemble with a distinctive profile is the Omnibus Wind Ensemble in Uppsala.

SYMPHONY ORCHESTRAS AND CHOIRS

Apart from the opera orchestras, Sweden's professional symphony orchestras include the Royal Stockholm Philharmonic Orchestra, the Swedish Radio Symphony Orchestra, and the Gothenburg National Symphony Orchestra as well as the symphony orchestras in Malmö, Norrköping, Helsingborg and Gävle.

CHOIRS

The Swedish Radio Choir and the Eric Ericson Chamber Choir (founded in 1945) have a well-established reputation as two of the world's leading mixed choirs and tour throughout the world. The choirs are also often asked to participate in international recordings. Other leading choirs include the Uppsala Academic Chamber Choir, the Hägersten Motet Choir, which is well-known on record but no longer in existence, the Adolf Fredrik Bach Choir and the male voice choir Orphei Drängar (the Sons of Orpheus) in Uppsala.

Swedish Opera Houses and Concert Venues

THE ROYAL OPERA (*Kungliga Teatern*) was founded by Gustav III in 1773. Operas had previously been performed in Stockholm by various foreign troupes as far back as the early 18th century. However, the king wished to establish a Swedish opera tradition with performances in the Swedish language. To begin with performances were staged at the Bollhuset theatre on Slottsbacken (demolished in 1792), after which activities were transferred to the new Gustavian Opera House in Gustav Adolfs Torg. It was designed by Carl Fredrik Adelcrantz as a twin building to the Palace of the Hereditary Prince (now the Foreign Office) on the opposite side of the same square. When the old Opera House became too small it was replaced in 1898 by the present Opera House, built on the same site and designed by Axel Anderberg. During various periods performances have also been given at several of the other theatres in the capital city. Notable conductors at the Royal Opera include the highly appreciated Finnish opera conductor Armas Järnefelt (1869–1958), who conducted the opera orchestra until 1932. The present principal conductor is Leif Segerstam, who was already attached to the Royal Opera in Stockholm from 1968 to 1972. He has also made frequent guest appearances. Walton Grönroos from the Finnish Åland islands is the present director of the Opera.

The Orchestra of the Royal Opera was founded as early as 1526 by King Gustav Vasa and was originally closely associated with the royal court. From the time of Gustav III the orchestra's main base has been the Royal Opera in Stockholm. For a long time it was the only professional orchestra in the capital city and also gave regular orchestral concerts before the forerunner of the present Stockholm Concert Hall Foundation was founded in 1902.

The equivalent to today's Royal Stockholm Philharmonic Orchestra was formed in 1914. From 1915 to 1924 the Finnish conductor Georg Schnéevoigt (1872–1947) was the orchestra's principal conductor and he came to play an important part in the orchestra's development (from 1930 to 1947 he was artistic director of the Malmö Concert Hall Orchestra). The present Concert Hall in Stockholm, designed by Ivar Tengbom, was inaugurated in 1926.

Concert institutions, concert halls and state-supported symphony orchestras were gradually established in several other towns. The Gothenburg Orchestral Society was formed as early as 1905 and the symphony orchestras in Gävle, Norrköping and Helsingborg were set up in the 1910s. The concert halls in Gothenburg (1935) and Helsingborg (1932) are particularly famous for their acoustics and functionalistic architecture.

In 1998 the Great Hall of the Royal Swedish Academy of Music, Sweden's oldest concert hall from 1878, was re-inaugurated under the auspices of the Swedish Concert Institute.

In its present size, with slightly more than a hundred members, the Swedish Radio Symphony Orchestra has been in existence since 1965, when the Radio Orchestra of that time was merged with the Light Orchestra. Sergiu Celibidache was the orchestra's conductor from 1962 to 1971 and he was responsible for raising it to an international level. Herbert Blomstedt was principal conductor from 1977 to 1982. The orchestra's most recent period of glory (which is still continuing) commenced in 1984/85, when the Finnish conductor Esa-Pekka Salonen was appointed principal conductor, a position which he held until 1995. The orchestra's permanent home is the Berwald Hall, inaugurated in 1979.

The Drottningholm Court Theatre is one of the world's best preserved 18th century theatres. Virtually the whole building, including the stage machinery, has remained untouched since its inauguration in 1766. Queen Lovisa Ulrika had the theatre built according to a design by Carl Fredrik Adelcrantz. The stage is still one of Sweden's deepest, with machinery which permits repeated speedy changes of scenery before an open curtain. The theatre's age of glory began in 1777 when Gustav III took over the Drottningholm Court. After the king's death in 1792 theatrical life stagnated and the Drottningholm Court Theatre sank into oblivion right up to the beginning of the 1920s when it was re-discovered by Arne Beijer. In 1922 the curtain rose again, and since then the Drottningholm Court Theatre has frequently been used for authentic productions and guest performances with works by composers such as Handel, Gluck, Haydn, Mozart and Rossini. Under Arnold Östman's direction period instruments became a matter of course.

The Gothenburg Opera House was inaugurated in 1994, replacing the Stora Theatre which was built in 1859 and which had been the only opera stage in the city since 1920. New opera companies, apart from those in Stockholm, Gothenburg and Malmö, include the Norrland Opera in Umeå, the Värmland Opera in Karlstad and the Vadstena Academy in Vadstena Castle which during the summer season specialises in Baroque opera and modern Swedish chamber operas.

The Folk Opera is a new opera company in Stockholm which often presents innovative and unconventional productions.

The Fylkingen Concert Society (formed in 1933 and now known as the Fylkingen Society for New Music and Intermedia Art) has played a significant part in promoting more innovative, experimental, boundary-crossing music, and the same is true of the electronic music studio *EMS*, which is now known under the name of Electro-Acoustic Music in Sweden. Since the 1960s *EMS* has produced several new generations of electronic music composers.

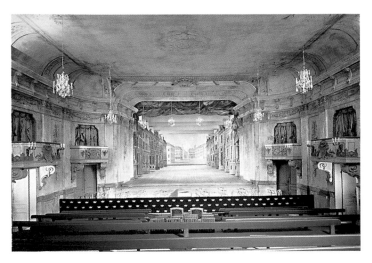

The Drottningholm Court Theatre. Photo: Bengt Wanselius.

Dalhalla, near Rättvik in central Sweden, one of the world's most spectacular natural stages. Swedish Concert Institute.

Berwald Concert Hall. Photo: Anders Roth/Sveriges Radio.

The Swedish Radio Symphony Orchestra. Photo: Mikael Strimhed.

The Gothenburg Opera. Photo: Ingmar Jernberg.

The Tambourine Studio in Malmö. Photo: Martin Bogren.

The Royal Opera. Photo: Mats Bäcker.

Folk Opera's production of "Marie Antoinette", music by Daniel Börtz, libretto by Claes Fellbom. Photo: Crimson Press.

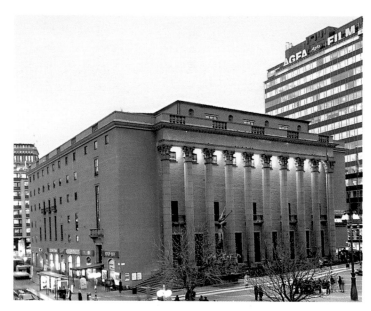

Stockholm Concert Hall. Photo: Gösta Nyberg.

A performance of "Baptism" with Kent Tankred och Leif Elggren at Fylkingen. Photo: Annika von Hauswolff.

Fasching—the home of jazz in Sweden. Photo: Tony Landberg.

The Great Hall of the Royal Swedish Academy of Music.
Swedish Concert Institute.

Useful Addresses

Royal Academy of Music *(Kungliga Musikaliska akademien)*, Stockholm
Tel: +46-8-611 57 20 Fax: +46-8-611 87 18 E-mail: adm@musakad.se

Swedish Concert Institute *(Rikskonserter)*, Stockholm
Tel: +46-8-407 16 00 Fax: +46-8-407 16 50 http://www.srk.se

Sveriges Radio, P2, Stockholm
Tel: +46-8-784 50 00 Fax: +46-8-667 37 01 http://www.sr.se

Sveriges Television, Stockholm
Tel: +46-8-784 00 00 Fax +46-8-784 15 00 http://www.svt.se

Royal Opera *(Kungliga Operan)*, Stockholm
Tel: +46-8-791 43 00 Fax: +46-8-650 82 30 http://www.kungligaoperan.se

Drottningholm Court Theatre *(Drottningholms Slottsteater)*, Stockholm
Tel: +46-8-665 14 00 Fax: +46-8-665 14 73
http://www.drottningholmsteatern.dtm.se

Folk Opera *(Folkoperan)*, Stockholm
Tel: +46-8-616 07 00 Fax: +46-8-84 41 46 http://www.folkoperan.se

Gothenburg Opera *(Göteborgs Operan)*, Göteborg
Tel: +46-31-10 80 00 Fax +46-31-10 80 30 http://www.opera.se

Malmö Musikteater, Malmö
Tel: +46-40-20 84 00 Fax: +46-40-20 84 23
http://www.malmomusikteater.se

Musikteatern i Värmland, Värmlandsoperan, Karlstad
Tel: +46-54-14 08 40 Fax: +46-54-10 05 33
http://www.musikteaternivarmland.se

Norrlandsoperan, Umeå
Tel: +46-90-15 43 00 Fax: +46-90-12 68 45, http://www.norrlandsoperan.se

Vadstena Academy *(Vadstena-Akademien)*, Stockholm
Tel: +46-8-652 61 80 Fax: +46-8-650 82 30
http://ourworld.compuserve.com/homepages/vadstak/

Royal Stockholm Philharmonic Orchestra *(Kungliga Filharmoniska Orkestern)*, Stockholm
Tel: +46-8-786 02 00 Fax: +46-8-791 73 30 http://www.konserthuset.se

Berwald Concert Hall *(Berwaldhallen)*
Tel: +46-8-784 50 00 Fax: +46-8-663 15 14 http://www.sr.se/berwaldhallen

Electroacoustic Music in Sweden *(EMS)* Stockholm
Tel: +46-8-658 19 90 Fax: +46-8-658 69 09 http://www.srk.se/ems

Fylkingen Society for New Music and Intermedia Art *(Fylkingen)*, Stockholm
Tel: +46-8-84 54 43 Fax: +46-8-669 38 68 http://www.fylkingen.se

Jazz club Fasching *(Fasching)*
Tel: +46-8-26 62 67 Fax: +46-8-21 04 34

Tambourine Studios, Malmö
Tel: +46-40-870 88 Fax: +46-40-870 80 http://www.vibrafon.se

Swedish Performing Rights Society *(STIM)*, Stockholm
Tel: +46-8-783 88 00 Fax: +46-8-662 62 75
http://www.stim.se http://www.mic.stim.se

Museum of Music *(Musikmuseet)*, Stockholm
Tel: +46-8-666 45 30 Fax: +46-8-663 91 81 http://www.musikmuseet.se

Svenska Musikfestivaler, Umeå
Tel: +46-90-14 25 80 Fax: +46-90-77 75 05
http://www.musikfestivaler.se

Falun Folkmusik Festival, Falun
Tel: +46-23-830 90 Fax: +46-23-633 99 http://www.falunfolkfest.se

Hultfredsfestivalen, Rockparty, Hultsfred
Tel: +46-495-695 00 Fax: +46-495-695 50 http://www.rockparty.se

THE SWEDISH CONCERT INSTITUTE (*Rikskonserter*) has an extensive mandate to organise and develop, on a national level, many vital areas of musical activity in Sweden.

The Swedish Concert Institute organises large numbers of concert tours annually, featuring both Swedish and international musicians, orchestras, choirs, and ensembles of all types. A wide spectrum of musical styles is represented ranging from chamber music and orchestras to folk music, world music and jazz.

Using government funding the Institute coordinates major music festivals, commissions new music and produces CD recordings on the Caprice Records label.

The well-known percussion ensemble Kroumata, the monthly magazine *Musik* and the electro-acoustic music centre, *EMS*, are also integral parts of the Swedish Concert Institute.

The Swedish Concert Institute now runs a beautifully restored 19th century concert hall in central Stockholm called Nybrokajen 11, where its offices are also located.

SWEDISH CONCERT INSTITUTE
Nybrokajen 11, SE-111 48 Stockholm, Sweden
Tel: + 46 8 407 16 00
Fax: +46 8 407 16 50
Internet address: http://www.srk.se

THE SWEDISH INSTITUTE *(Svenska institutet)* is a public agency established to disseminate knowledge abroad about Sweden's social and cultural life, to promote cultural and informational exchange with other countries and to contribute to increased international cooperation in the fields of education and research. The Swedish Institute produces a wide range of publications on many aspects of Swedish society. These publications can be obtained directly from the Swedish Institute or from Swedish diplomatic missions abroad.

In the SWEDEN BOOKSHOP you will find—in several foreign languages—books, brochures, fact sheets and richly illustrated gift books on Sweden, a broad selection of Swedish fiction and children's books as well as Swedish music, slides, video cassettes and Swedish language courses.

VISIT THE SWEDEN BOOKSHOP

Sweden House at Hamngatan/Kungsträdgården

in Stockholm

PHONE ORDER DEPARTMENT

+46-8-789 20 00

WRITE TO THE SWEDISH INSTITUTE

Box 7434, SE-103 91 Stockholm, Sweden

Fax: +46-8-20 72 48

Internet address: http://www.si.se

E-mail: order@si.se